Woodlawn

A HISTORY

Woodlawn

A HISTORY

WOODLAWN HERITAGE GROUP
EDITED BY BERNADETTE DOHERTY

First published 2016

The History Press Ireland
50 City Quay
Dublin 2
Ireland
www.thehistorypress.ie

The History Press Ireland is a member of Publishing Ireland,
the Irish book publishers' association.

British Library Cataloguing in Publication Data.
A catalogue record for this book is available from the British Library.

ISBN 978 1 84588 907 4

Typesetting and origination by The History Press

CONTENTS

PREFACE

Woodlawn Heritage Group was formed in 1993, based on an idea of the late Paddy Quinn, Killaan, Woodlawn. Unfortunately, Paddy passed away before his idea came to fruition. Following an invitation from Tom McLoughlin to a group of interested local people, the inaugural meeting of Woodlawn Heritage Group was held on 26 January that year. Elected officers at that meeting were Tom McLoughlin, president; Tom Seale, chairperson; Alf Seale, vice-chairman; Tom Byrne, treasurer; Anne-Marie Byrne, secretary.

The general aim of the group was to develop and preserve the amenities of the Woodlawn area. As a means of having development and preservation work carried out, it was decided that the group would sponsor a Community Employment Scheme. Over many years, the group undertook various conservation projects on a number of the heritage buildings in the area, restoring stonewalls and towers and enhancing the general landscape.

Nigh on ten years ago, it was noted by the group that no comprehensive history of Woodlawn had ever been published. The idea of the group producing this history remained on the agenda for many years until, finally, in the year 2009, a sub-committee was formed to take charge of this project. This committee comprised Des Doherty (chairman), Angela Magennis (secretary), Paul Quinn, Tom Seale, Alf Seale, Michael John Kilgannon, Mary Gorman, Maeve Raftery, Celsus Sheridan, Marian Kenny, Tom and Anne-Marie Byrne, Nicola Hampson, and Eileen Kelly, RIP.

With so many enthusiastic people involved, one would imagine that the book would have been on the shelves in a matter of months; little did we know what we were letting ourselves in for! The path to this book has taken many twists and has been an education to everyone involved. We soon realised that we needed some professional assistance and engaged the services of Sheelagh Conway, a local published author, under the auspices of Tús initiative. Sheelagh gave some insightful workshops to the committee on how to decide on chapter format and content, interviewing and editing techniques. We are also grateful to Declan Kelly, a native of Ballinasloe and the author of several published books, for his insight and contribution to this publication.

The committee also undertook a 'Localore' course conducted by Tomas Hardiman, co-ordinated by Marie Mannion, Heritage Officer of Galway County Council, and funded by Galway Rural Development (GRD). This course provided valuable information on methods of researching historical and photographic archives together with recording local spoken histories, and was of enormous benefit to all participants.

The path took another twist with the arrival of Bernadette Doherty, archaeologist, as a participant on the Community Employment Scheme in April 2013. She was initially recruited as a researcher on the archaeology of Woodlawn and its hinterlands, but her many talents were soon evident and she became the main driving force in finally getting this book to publication. Bernadette was ably assisted by Marian Deely, who joined the CE scheme in July 2014.

Due to the sheer quantity of quality material researched and gathered, it became obvious that it could not all be included in one volume. Difficult decisions had to be made regarding where to begin and end. Also due to publishing restraints, we were obliged to concentrate on historical, fact-based material for this volume. We are hopeful to produce a series of journals made up of the remainder of the material as a sequel to this book.

We therefore present to you the collective efforts of the Woodlawn Heritage Group, the Book Committee and all our knowledgeable contributors, in what we believe to be an informative and readable history of Woodlawn.

We hope you enjoy it.

Des Doherty, chairman
Angela Magennis, secretary
woodlawn.galwaycommunityheritage.org

ACKNOWLEDGMENTS

The Woodlawn Heritage Group would like to acknowledge and thank the following for their assistance and contributions:

Des Doherty, Angela Magennis, Paul Quinn, Marian Kenny, Celsus Sheridan, Alf Seale, Tom Seale, Brigid Seale, Maeve Raftery, Nicola Hampson, Eileen Kelly (RIP), Anne-Marie Byrne, Tom Byrne, Mary Gorman, Michael John Kilgannon, Maureen Kilgannon, Bríd Mercer, Marie Mannion (heritage officer, Galway County Council), Galway Rural Development, Sheelagh Conway, Shiela Counihan, Tomas Hardiman, Declan Kelly, Bernadette Doherty, Sean Broderick, Carrie O'Sullivan, Marian Deely, Gerry Mullins, Eimear Quinn, Anne Carey, Christy Cunniffe, Rita O'Neill, Nelly Mentane, Chris Doherty, Justin Mitchell, Michael Daly, Brigie Kelly, Joe Keane, The Cannon Family, Ann Earles, Roderick Ashtown, Mary Dempsey, Mary Sheridan, Ballymacward Hall Committee, Irish Historical Group, staff members of Loughrea Library, Galway City Library HO, National Archives, National Library of Ireland, Science Museum Group Enterprises Ltd, Bradford, staff and pupils of Woodlawn National School, Fr Pat Kenny PP, Fr Raymond Sweeney, National Monuments Service, Cultural Resource Development Services Ltd (CRDS), National Roads Authority (NRA), Angela Gallagher, Archaeology Department and James Hardiman Library at the National University of Ireland, Galway (NUIG), Bill Grealish.

WOODLAWN HERITAGE GROUP – CURRENT MEMBERS

Maeve Fahy (president), Agnes Cannon and Joy Donoghue (life hon members), Paul Quinn (chairman), Des Doherty (vice-chairman), Maeve Raftery (secretary), Marian Kenny (treasurer), Mary Gorman PRO, Justin Mitchell (director CE Scheme), Michael J. Kilgannon (director CE Scheme).

Angela Magennis, Michael Daly, Celsus Sheridan, Joe and Anne Coyne, Rita O'Neill, Judy McDonagh, Chris Doherty, Terry and John Hanlon, Tom Seale, Michael Mullins, Nicola and Derek Hampson, Alf and Ida Seale.

Woodlawn Heritage Group celebrate on winning 'The Golden Mile Award', 2006.

INTRODUCTION

I first became aware of Woodlawn in the mid-1960s. I was a student in California when I was given a slim volume of poems by Bob Ashtown, the fourth holder of the title 'Lord Ashtown'. The poem that caught my eye was entitled 'My Happy Childhood Days 1902–1912': in its lines, Bob recalls his idyllic upbringing at Woodlawn:

> Of all the great estates I've known
> I loved the best, I proudly own,
> My old ancestral Irish home
> So blest in bygone days!
>
> At Woodlawn I such freedom won
> As seldom comes to any son,
> (except a very privileged one)
> No matter where he strays.
>
> *Poems by Lord Ashtown* (Dolmen Press Ltd, 1965)

He goes on to recount his growing love of nature and his introduction to shooting and fishing, all of which were to remain his passions for the remainder of his life. The closing date of the poem is of significance as that was the year in which his father, Frederick Oliver Trench, the 3rd Baron, was declared bankrupt and the retention of Woodlawn hung in the balance for a number of years. Things were never going to be the same again. Ten years later an auction took place at the house. It lasted for three days, and virtually all the contents of the house were sold, down to the linoleum on the floor, but for some reason or other the family subsequently decided to remain in Ireland and carried on living at Woodlawn in much-reduced circumstances. It was not until 1947, following the death of his father the previous year, that Bob Ashtown was forced to sell the estate after paying heavy death and succession duties.

My first visit to Woodlawn was in 1983, when I came over to Ireland with my father and my son, Timothy. I vividly remember my father's reaction at seeing the state of the house, which had been empty then for about ten years. He was visibly upset and we did not stay long. I do not think that he ever went back to the house on his subsequent trips to Ireland although he did visit the mausoleum. On one occasion he was at the station and met a man called Jim Kett, who had worked as a signalman there for many years. He asked him for directions to the mausoleum where the Ashtowns were buried. 'Lord Ashtown is dead for many years,' Jim replied, whereupon my father answered, much to Jim's surprise, 'No he's not. You're looking at him!'

My own personal involvement with Woodlawn did not really begin until 1999. My father had inherited the title in 1990 from a cousin in Canada and in 1999 he received a letter from a distant relative informing him of the dire state of the Ashtown Mausoleum. As he had suffered a stroke in 1996, he no longer able to travel so I volunteered to go over to see what, if anything, could be done to salvage this unusual monument in the depths of East Galway. It was on this trip that I first made the acquaintance of Tom Seale, who in the ensuing years has been of such enormous help and support in maintaining and caring for our family burial ground.

The result of my visit was that I started to investigate the possibility of obtaining a grant to help with the restoration of the mausoleum. Fortunately at that time grant money was still readily available and with the help of Gerry McManus, a conservation architect from Claregalway, we managed to obtain generous funding from both the Heritage Council and Galway County Council of more than €25,000, which my father and I had to match. The work was carried out expertly by the local firm of Thomas Mitchell & Sons and was their last major project. It was completed by the end of 2002. The transformation was better than could have been hoped for. I was fortunate again in 2014 to receive a further grant of €6,000, which we used to stabilise the tower in the centre of the mausoleum. Hopefully no further work will be necessary in my lifetime and I look forward to being laid to rest there in due course!

The restoration of the mausoleum inspired me to delve deeper into our family history and our connections not only with the Woodlawn area, but also with other places in Ireland where the Trench family owned houses and estates. The past fifteen years have produced a great deal of new information on the family and led me to meet many interesting people from the Woodlawn area as well as Dublin, Limerick, Tipperary and NUI Maynooth. I have been fortunate to have been able to visit and sometimes stay in houses such as Sopwell Hall in Tipperary and Castle Oliver in Limerick. I discovered, among many other things, that we still had fishing rights along much of the River Nire in Waterford, as the river ran through the Glenaheiry Estate, which had been purchased by the 2nd Lord Ashtown in 1876. I am now in the process of returning these rights to the local angling clubs because I feel that is the way things should be these days. The research carried out by myself and others, notably Professor Perry Curtis and Bríd Mercer, has resulted in articles (not written by myself, I hasten to add) appearing in several learned journals over the past ten years. Although some of the information unearthed did not always portray the family in a good light, I have never been one to shy away from the truth and have no desire to whitewash the family history. In fact being objective has often made the journey more interesting and led me to understand Ireland and her history far better than I did when I started out.

I have tried to keep interest in the fate of Woodlawn House alive as far as possible and was very pleased when Tarquin Blake put the house on the cover of *Abandoned Mansions of Ireland*, Vol. 2, published in 2013. Tarquin kindly let me proofread his piece on the house in the book and I can therefore vouch for its accuracy on the family history.

Following my father's death in March 2010 we brought his ashes over to be interred in the mausoleum. The service was held in Woodlawn church on 19 May and to our surprise the church was packed, although very few people would have known him personally. My son, Timothy, gave the eulogy. Recalling our 1983 visit to Woodlawn he said:

Despite being visibly upset at seeing the big house abandoned, I remember being surprised at how relaxed and comfortable he seemed being here. Ireland was in a sense 'home' during all his travelling and his life in London. He visited his uncle and cousin in Tipperary regularly from the 1950s to the 1970s when on leave and kept up correspondence with people here until the early '90s.

So it is to Ireland he has returned. He made one previous visit to the Mausoleum, clambering over the gate to get in I believe, before the place had been restored. I am sure he would be very surprised to see all these faces here this morning; he was a shy and modest man, I think, and certainly never boastful. He was like us all, a person of his times.

Even though I have never lived in Ireland, I too feel relaxed when I come over here and especially when I turn the corner at Killaan Crossroads and see the big house sitting up on the hill. A few years ago, someone in Woodlawn, unfortunately I cannot remember who it was, paid me the greatest compliment when they said that they would look forward to seeing me the next time that I was 'home'.

Finally I would like to express my admiration for the Woodlawn Heritage Group and the contributors to this publication for all the research and hard work that have gone into producing this book. It is proof of what can be achieved by a small rural community, who have dedicated their time and energy to the area in which they live and love.

Roderick Trench, 8th Baron Ashtown
March 2015

Roderick Trench is the 8th holder of the title 'Lord Ashtown of Moate', which was granted to his ancestor Frederick Trench, MP for Portarlington, in 1800. Born in 1944, he was educated at Eton College and Stanford University in California. He spent some years working at the Foreign Office in London before training to be a TEFL (teaching English as a foreign language) teacher and spent most of his career in Eastbourne on the south-east coast of England. During the past twenty years he has become increasingly interested in the history of his family in Ireland and tries to visit the Woodlawn area every year. He is married with two children and lives in East Sussex in the UK.

Trench Mausoleum.
(Recorded Monument
GA73:143)

A NOTE ON THE AUTHORS

ANNE CAREY is an archaeologist and a historic buildings specialist, based in Galway city. She has conducted research into the conservation of masonry monuments in State care and worked throughout Ireland on developer-led conservation projects. Her interests include buildings of Woodlawn estate, urban settlement and church buildings from all periods. Anne is originally from Ballygar, County Galway.

CHRISTY CUNNIFFE is an archaeology graduate of NUI Galway. He currently works as the Field Monument Advisor for Galway County Council. He has a special interest in the archaeology of the medieval Irish church. He is currently recording the archaeology of early modern settlement in the Slieve Aughty region.

MARIAN DEELY is researcher and assistant editor with the Woodlawn Heritage Group. Originally from north Cork, she worked in America for a number of years before returning to her home town where she worked for an American company. She moved to Loughrea in 1995. Settled in East Galway, she is living with her husband Sean and their three children, Ciara, Cleona and Chloe, in Galboley, Bullaun, Loughrea.

BERNADETTE DOHERTY is an archaeologist and graduate of University College Galway (now NUIG). Having worked extensively throughout Ireland, she settled in East Galway and worked with a private consultancy. Initially employed with Woodlawn Heritage as a researcher, she proceeded to edit this publication. Originally from Donegal, she lives with her husband Tony and their two children Liam and Áine May in Carra, Bullaun, Loughrea.

DES DOHERTY is fifth-generation native to Woodlawn through his paternal grandparents. His mother was the postmistress at Woodlawn post office, having bought the premises that was formerly a gate lodge to Woodlawn House in 1954. Des was born in Woodlawn and is still living in that house with his wife, Christine, who is the current postmistress. Des also worked for An Post for twenty-three years in different grades. He is on the Sponsor Committee of the local Community Employment Scheme and is vice-chairman of Woodlawn Heritage Group. Des and Christine have four children, Lisa, Kevin, Drew and Orla, all of whom attended Woodlawn National School.

MARY GORMAN grew up in Ballinlough, Woodlawn with her parents Dan and Nora Carney, brothers Pat and Joe and sister Kathleen. She emigrated to Lancashire, England in 1970 where she qualified as a nurse and later went to London to continue her nursing career. Mary returned to Carrowmore, Woodlawn in 2007 where she now lives with her husband Eamonn. She is an active member of the Woodlawn Heritage Group.

MICHAEL JOHN KILGANNON is a retired school teacher and active member of the Woodlawn Heritage Group. Born in Liscune to parents William and Brigid (*née* Nutley), Michael John trained as a National School teacher and worked in Cloonkeenkerril, Esker and Ballymacward National Schools. He is married to Maureen (*née* Connolly) and they have six adult children: Bríd, Irene, Micheal, Padraig, Brian and Catherine.

BRÍD MERCER is a freelance proofreader and editor. She is the daughter of Michael John and Maureen Kilgannon and grew up in Tullawicky, Woodlawn but now lives in England. She has previously published material on Woodlawn in the 2011 *Journal of the Galway Archaeological and Historical Society*. She is continuing her research on Woodlawn and can be contacted at tullawicky@ btinternet.com.

GERRY MULLINS attended University College Cork as a mature student in order to study archaeology and history. Having graduated with a BA he continued to study archaeology and received a First-Class Honours MA. Following that, he spent several years working on archaeological excavations throughout Ireland as both an assistant archaeologist and excavation supervisor before passing his licence-eligibility interview. He later directed archaeological excavations on several sites including the Hillfort at Rahally and the multi-period burial ground at neighbouring Cross. Gerry is currently teaching archaeology, history and cultural heritage courses at Pearse College of Further Education, Clogher Road, Crumlin. He lives with his wife, Leonie, near Monamolin, County Wexford.

EIMEAR QUINN is a graduate of NUIG. Her MA thesis in history 'The Barons of Ashtown and the Woodlawn Estate, 1850–1923' was written under the supervision of Dr John Cunningham. She grew up in Cloonacallis, Woodlawn with parents Paul and Patricia, sister Eibhlín and brother Eoin. She is currently teaching in Scoil Chonglais, in Baltinglass, County Wicklow.

TOM SEALE is one of five children born to Alfred and Mary (*née* Echlan). He attended Woodlawn National School for eight years, graduating with a Primary Certificate. He has always lived in Woodlawn, commuting to various locations throughout the county for employment. He is now retired and living with his wife Brigid. They have five children who all attended Woodlawn National School.

1

PREHISTORIC WOODLAWN

BERNADETTE DOHERTY

The Old Stone Age (Palaeolithic) saw bands of people hunting throughout Europe and Britain. These were a primitive people, living hand-to-mouth. There is no evidence to date for the Palaeolithic in Ireland, but as M. Ryan suggests in his book *Irish Archaeology Illustrated*, perhaps we just haven't been looking for it![1] It is true that the last great Ice Age would have destroyed much of the evidence. As human beings, we naturally preserve only what we know to be precious; for some this is something with an immediate association with other people, and the places we hold dear. It is the responsibility of all of us to help preserve and protect our landscape and heritage. However small a contribution, the effect shall impact on the lives of generations that come after us.

ESKER RIADA

The social history of Ireland, indeed of East Galway is as the man says as old as the hills. The Woodlawn area is remarkable in its landscape with its rich deposit of an esker ridge that once spanned the country in an east–west orientation. Known as the *Slighe Mhór*, the Esker Riada provided the natural dry route through bogs, wetlands and woods for centuries. This route has been used again and again, until even in the last few decades the ridge was exploited to provide materials for the construction of our newer thoroughfares.

An esker is a natural deposit formed when ice melted during a period of glacial retreat. The last Irish glacial maximum occurred approximately 18,000 years ago, the ice retreating some 6 to 8,000 years later. The remains of the esker ridge are visible outside New Inn. It is most obvious to the passer by on the Ballinasloe road to the east of New Inn, particularly where a house truncates the ridge.

The humpback hills within this somewhat flat landscape are another feature of glacial landform. Drumlins are between 25 and 50m high, kames are usually less than 30m high. As naturally dry areas within a marshy and wet landscape, these areas have been harnessed for centuries by man. The settlements located on the surface of these hills are testament to centuries of archaeology in the area.

Prehistory in Ireland is divided into four key phases: Mesolithic, Neolithic, Bronze Age and Iron Age. The Bronze Age is sub-divided into a further three phases: Early, Middle and Late Bronze Age.

MESOLITHIC (8000–4000 BC)

Mesolithic comes from *meso*, meaning middle and *lithic*, meaning stone. Mesolithic sites in Ireland are rare, yet we have learned a great deal to date about the culture of our earliest foragers and hunters. There are no known Mesolithic sites in East Galway to date, but the occurrence of a number of significant Mesolithic finds indicate a presence in the area. Mesolithic finds were retrieved from excavations associated with a Bronze Age site at Urraghry, Ballinasloe.[2] The site comprised a burnt mound and trough with fifteen stake-holes, as well as a palaeochannel and gully. Charcoal from the site yielded two Early Bronze Age radiocarbon dates. These Mesolithic finds, although not in context, would suggest human activity in the area prior to these dates.

Recent storm damage to our coastal regions resulted in the discovery of a number of Mesolithic stone axe heads along the Connemara coastline.[3] Discoveries by the general public are key to pinpointing sites and locations of possible prehistoric activity. Stray finds are an indication of the archaeological importance of an area.

Professor Woodman excavated a number of significant sites in the 1970s and 1990s in Counties Derry and Kerry.[4] Lough Boora, near Birr in Offaly and more recent excavations in Limerick have added to our understanding of the first people on this island.

Mount Sandel in Derry revealed an occupation area containing several circular huts. The postholes were slanted in a way that would suggest saplings were put in the ground in a circle and tied together at the top, creating a curved or dome-shaped structure. These were presumably covered with hide or other material that left no trace. Excavations revealed this site was re-used over and over again, suggesting it was a seasonal location for camping. However, all the seasons were represented in the remains: spring and summer were indicated by the large number of salmon bones and autumn by hazelnut shells; winter occupation was suggested by foetal pig bone. There was also evidence for a tool-making industry with remnants of flint and chert cores and microliths. These people made tools for hunting and defending themselves. In Lough Boora in Offaly a stone assemblage was retrieved indicative of a similar technique of production as found at Mount Sandel, characteristic of the period 7000–5500 BC. This site was revealed on a gravel ridge when a lake was drained for the production of turf in a bog.[5]

We know the Mesolithic people practiced funerary ceremonies as revealed at Hermitage, County Limerick.[6] On the banks of the River Shannon, a group of people gathered and camped next to the ultimate source of food and transportation. Excavations here revealed token burials of burnt bone deposited into graves. One grave was originally marked with a post. A large stone axe was found in association with the burial remains, along with a number of flint and chert artefacts. The axe had evidence of burning, which suggested that it had also been placed on the funerary pyre. As only a token amount of the burnt bone was deposited in this way, it is suggested that the remains of the bone may have been disposed of in the River Shannon.[7] Radiocarbon dating retrieved the earliest known date for funerary practices in this country (7530– 7320 BC). Another grave located some 100m away was from a later date (7090–7030 BC). This was a larger pit, with no grave marker, and contained the remains of a male. A funeral pyre was also located at this site.

NEOLITHIC (4000–2500 BC)

The Neolithic period (*neo* meaning late and *lithic* meaning stone) in Ireland is associated with the introduction of farming. Hunting and gathering is still a main source of sustenance, and the use of stone tools continues. However, animal husbandry begins to emerge, tillage farming is introduced and the clearance of trees gives way to complex field systems. A great example of these are the Ceide Fields in County Mayo.

Excavations of Neolithic houses have revealed the remains of structures that would have required people to invest time and energy in their construction. Large rectangular buildings of split oak planks, possibly with thatch roofs, are represented in excavations by deep slot trenches. Large postholes represent the partitions within these houses, and may have supported a second floor, or attic space. The quality of these structures suggests a more stable lifestyle, a move from the mobile existence of the Mesolithic man. The introduction of pottery is evident as is the use of saddle querns for grinding corn. The emergence of some of the most substantial megalithic tombs shows us a people with reverence for the afterlife.

A Neolithic stone axe was discovered amongst the many lithics found out of context during the nearby excavation at Rahally.[8] This would suggest that there was occupation in the area prior to the construction of the hillfort in the Bronze Age.

MEGALITHIC TOMBS

There are three basic varieties of megalithic (*mega* meaning large and *lithic* meaning stone) tombs in Ireland: the court tomb, the passage tomb and the portal tomb. A fourth, the Linkardstown type, is a large stone cist burial within a mound, predominantly found in the southern half of the country. Court and portal tombs are variants of the same funerary tradition, closely linked with our early farmers. It is believed that these large stone tombs

Annagh burial mound. (Recorded Monument GA73:007, photograph courtesy of the National Monuments Service Photographic Unit)

evolved from a wooden prototype that would have been covered with earthen mounds. The court tomb is generally found in the northern half of the country. Its most distinctive feature is the oval or U-shaped roofless courtyard set in front of a gallery (burial chamber). Burial chambers often contain grave goods such as unglazed pottery, flint and/or chert tools. Portal tombs are characterised by a simpler design, based on a tripod plan. Single slabs resting against the portals and a backstone form the chamber sides. An upright slab placed between the portals and backstone may seal the entrance to the chamber. One of the most famous portal tombs in the country is Poulnabrone in the Burren, County Clare. Both portal and court tombs are typically found in low-lying land.

Recorded Monument GA73:007 (burial mound) located in the townland of Annagh is described as an unclassified tomb. It is marked on the OSI maps as 'stones'. The Archaeological Inventory of County Galway, Vol. 2 describes it as an 'Unclassified Tomb'.[9] The supporting stones are most certainly natural but the 'capstone' has been placed there deliberately. It is approximately 1.5m long and 0.70m wide and is perforated with small holes. Other large stones litter the surrounding field walls, which may have been part of the present structure. The mound was 5.5m high and had a diameter of 35m. It is recorded that a number of bones were recovered from the inside of the cist. Today, this monument is barely visible to the passer-by as it is overgrown.

BRONZE AGE (2500–500 BC)

It is the introduction of metallurgy that outlines the most significant change in Irish society during this period. The Later Neolithic Period and the Early Bronze Age merge while there is gradual change in the day-to-day living. Farming remains the main focus for the economy, with stone tools and implements continuing in use. Bronze Age pottery is more refined than the course ware of the Neolithic period. The houses become circular or annular in plan. They are defined by slot trenches cut into clay, and vary in size. Some have annexes or porches attached. There is little evidence for hearths within these houses, suggesting a preference to cooking outside. The emergence of *fulachta fiadh* in this period would support this view. There is a move to the higher ground, and we see the first instance of hilltop enclosures (evidence of such at Rahally to the south of Woodlawn; see forthcoming article by Gerry Mullins). These larger enclosures may signify the emergence of a social hierarchy, or political unrest.

FULACHTA FIADH

A typical and most common feature of the Irish Bronze Age is the *fulachta fiadh*. Although there are none recorded to date in the Record of Monuments and Places for the immediate area of Woodlawn, this landscape would be quite typical for this type of monument. It can be recognised as a horseshoe or kidney-shaped mound of burnt stone close to a water source. A vast number of these sites have been discovered in the last number of decades, and new evidence has shown that they were not only used for bathing or cooking, but also for dying and even brewing. Constructed by digging a trough into the ground, the hole may have been lined with stone or wood. The trough was then filled with water from a nearby water source. This water was then heated and brought to boiling point by throwing hot rocks into the trough. The rocks would split and break, hence the mound of burnt stones left in the wake of its use. It is the burnt mound that is recognisable in our low-lying, marshy landscape. Charcoal-rich soil may be noticed in freshly ploughed fields, or a concentration of fire-cracked stone within a peaty or marshy area could indicate the site of a *fulachta fiadh*. Excavations associated with the construction of the M6 motorway uncovered a number of these sites at Caraun More, Treenbaun and Killescragh.[10]

METAL PRODUCTION

The introduction of metals to Irish society came as a result of exchange with British and European societies. It would take time for Ireland's inhabitants to develop the skills and knowledge of mining, smelting and casting required to impact on the country as a whole. The earliest metals were copper and gold, and then an alloy bronze. Copper mining is evident from excavations at Mount Gabriel in County Cork. Excavations retrieved wood and charcoal from this site which was dated to 1700–1500 BC, which makes these the oldest copper mines in North-West Europe. Natural deposits were not common throughout the country, which meant that the prehistoric metal worker had to extract from ores. This required the development of an industry organising a large number of people to supply the manpower, and would suggest a highly intelligent and organised society in the Bronze Age. Smelting required high, intense heat, which was obtained by burning large quantities of wood from the forests. Bronze Age men would have used the stone axe at first, then in time they developed the bronze flat axe which would prove to be twice as efficient at tree felling as the lithic original. Our first industrial revolution would have its own impact on the environment. The intense felling of trees from the forests meant large areas became waterlogged. Over time the boglands that we are familiar with today were produced. Peat by its nature helped to preserve some of our country's greatest finds.

EARLY BRONZE AGE STRAY FIND

The earliest recorded activity in the immediate Woodlawn area is documented by the stray find of a bronze halberd from Cloonymorris. The halberd was presented to the museum in September 1948 by the then-National School teacher, Mrs Elizabeth Mulvihill. Mrs Mulvihill, in a letter to the museum, explained how this weapon was found by Mr Richard Mullen while he was cutting turf in his bog at Cloonymorris, Woodlawn. The bog had never been cut before, and the discovery was made some 5 feet from the surface of the bog. This type of halberd belongs to the Early Bronze Age, dating from 1800 to 1400 BC, although it has also been found in later contexts.

A halberd is a broad-shaped blade with a strong mid-rib that has been described as resembling the beak of a crane. It would have been mounted onto a wooden shaft at a right angle, and was invented in order to shield more effectively than could be done with a spear. The Cloonymorris halberd is classified as an O'Riordain, Type 5.

There has been a vast quantity of Bronze Age weapons found in wetland areas, lakes and shorelines throughout the country. Hoards of copper, bronze and gold have been retrieved in bogs, lakes and rivers, some of which may have been part of votive offerings to the gods, and others might have been placed there to be stored for a later time, or hidden from pillagers. The fact that the Cloonymorris halberd was a single find would indicate it was hidden until required again, or simply lost en route through the bog. A recent article has made reference to the possibility that the halberd may have been used in ritualistic dancing.[11] Rock carvings in Sweden and northern Italy have reproduced the image of the halberd, showing its popularity throughout the continent. One such carving at Mount Bego, Italy, shows a number of people holding halberds in what appears to be a ritualised fight or dance.

The Cloonymorris Halberd. (Reg No P1948:105, photograph reproduced courtesy of the National Museum of Ireland)

These drawings show the halberd looking remarkably like the beak, head and neck of the crane. This is not at all surprising, as the crane has been associated with Irish mythology, druids and royalty throughout the ages. It was deemed a sin to eat the flesh of the crane, and this bird's mating ritual dance has been copied by druids to the present day.

The crane, although now extinct some 300 years, would have been a very common sight in the Woodlawn area. The Gaelic *an gCorr* refers to the 'korrrrr' sound or cry the bird made. This may be represented in the townland name of Corskeagh, north-west of Woodlawn. Today, its close cousin, the heron, can be seen along the rivers of this low-lying land.

MOYARWOOD SPEARHEAD

Another find from this era is a spear found at Moyarwood. Discovered during the cutting of turf by the county council in 1946, it was found at a depth of around 150cm; according to the finder a small iron knife was found with the spearhead (this has been mislaid). Mitchell (1950/51) describes the profile of the peat in which the spear was found to be within a 'Molinia Peat with little evidence of re-generation structure and resembling in general blanket-bog peat rather than raised bog peat'.[12]

The find is described as a leaf-shaped spearhead, measuring 232mm in length, 62mm maximum width. Asymmetrically placed lunate openings occur in the blade; there is a small circular perforation above one opening and below another. There are peg holes in the socket immediately below the blade; the socket mouth is of hexagonal cross-section. Socketed spearheads like this were cast in complex moulds with a plug to form the socket, a technology introduced late in the Earlier Bronze Age. The earlier spearhead was a flat, dagger-like blade with a tang that would have been mounted onto a wooden shaft. The socketed form, like that of Moyarwood, would have been a much stronger implement in battle. It is impossible to say why this implement was

Moyarwood Spearhead, currently in the care of NUIG. It was found in a bog 1946.
(Photographed by B. Doherty with kind permission of Archaeology Department, NUIG)

deposited in the bog. Was it a ceremonial deposition? Was it misplaced? Was it hidden for future use? The iron knife found with the spearhead never made it to the university. The site was inspected after these objects were discovered, but no archaeological features were found to be associated with the spearhead.

IRON AGE (500 BC– AD 400)

The introduction of iron tools and weapons and a definite artistic style for this period are what emerge from our repository of artefacts distinguishing a new age of people. There is the continuation of the use of bronze and gold for jewellery, but it is the distinctive La Tène ornamental artwork that we associate with the Iron Age. This culture or influence came from mainland Europe, and on the cusp of the written historical record there are many references to these people as a fearsome and barbaric lot. A number of significant sites of ceremonial status emerge within this period including Emain Macha (Navan Fort) County Armagh, Dún Ailinne, County Kildare and Cruachain, County Roscommon.[13] Again, Rahally has an association with the Iron Age.

The Turoe Stone, located at Turoe House, Bullaun (currently removed from Bullaun to be restored) is a significant emblem of the Iron Age. Decorated in relief carvings of leaf and bird motifs, this is one of a number of such monoliths in the country. Castlestrange, County Roscommon, Derrykeighan, County Antrim and Killycluggin, County Cavan all are fine examples of technical expertise and skill. The Turoe Stone in particular is described as the work of a master mason, with its quadripartite ornament and false-relief design. The stone itself is of granite, and measures 1.68m (5ft 6in) in height. This decoration is also seen in metalworking and on swords and scabbards of the same era.

The Turoe Stone was originally located at Feerwore Rath, the site of a ringfort, and taken to Turoe House by the Dunlop family in the 1850s. The original location of the stone is still somewhat dubious. It was identified that the original position of the stone was some '10 yards to the west of the ringfort'.[14] Excavation in the 1940s did not investigate the possible original location for the stone. It was recorded that two smaller stones were also associated with the ringfort at Feerwore.

Another phenomenon of this period is the deposition of bodies in bogs. A number of bog bodies were discovered in the last few decades throughout the country during the cutting of turf. It would appear these were sacrificial killings, as research shows that the victims were of special status and wealth.

This has led to the suggestion by Kelly that they may have been failed kings or failed candidates for kingship.[15] In the townland of Cloonahinch, north of Woodlawn Station, a pair of human feet was discovered in June 1972. The remains were apparently found close to the base of a bog hole. It is possible the feet were the only surviving part of a more ancient bog body which had been exposed and dispersed over years through turf cutting.[16]

The prehistoric presence of man in the Woodlawn area has only been touched upon here. Our landscape is unique in that the archaeology in this area is so well preserved, and we already have a vast amount visible to us in our everyday surroundings. The forthcoming paper by Gerry Mullins is a fantastic example of how archaeological investigations can expand our knowledge of the everyday lives of the people who came before us. What appears to be a mere hump or bump in a field beside your home could well be another monument waiting to be discovered. We need not fear the unknown, but respect what is ours for only a short moment in time.

'A true conservationist is a man who knows that the world is not given by his fathers, but borrowed from his children.'

John James Audubon

2

RAHALLY: AN EXCAVATION ON YOUR DOORSTEP

GERRY MULLINS

Archaeological excavations were undertaken at Rahally prior to the construction of the M6 Galway to East Ballinasloe road scheme which began in 2007. Due to the location of a bivallate ringfort (GA86:211)[17] immediately outside the road corridor to the south and two undated field system banks (GA86:213) partly within, testing of the area was initially undertaken by Martin Jones (excavation 03E1871) and Jerry O'Sullivan (excavation 04E0803).[18] Both recommended further investigation. Subsequent archaeological testing and excavations were undertaken by Cultural Resource Development Services Ltd (CRDS Ltd) at the request of Galway County Council (ministerial directions reference nos A024/3.9 and A024/3.8). Rahally townland is situated near the village of New Inn (*An Cnoc Breac*) in east County Galway in the civil parish of Grange, the barony of Kilconnell. The site was situated on a hillside with a northern aspect, in pastureland, about 1.75km south-east of the Raford River (NGR 166007 225872; height between 97m OD and 104m OD; excavation reg. no. E2006; phases 1 and 2 excavations were undertaken under ministerial directions nos A024/008 and A041). Rahally hill forms part of a glacial ridge with lower wet pasture and marshland occurring to the south and north-east.

When the archaeological team first entered the fields at Rahally to undertake this work, there was no expectation that they were about to uncover evidence of human activities in the area spanning over 3,000 years. Among the previously unknown archaeological monuments revealed were a prehistoric hillfort, an early medieval annex to the preserved bivallate ringfort, a second early medieval ringfort and an early modern stone-lined drying kiln.

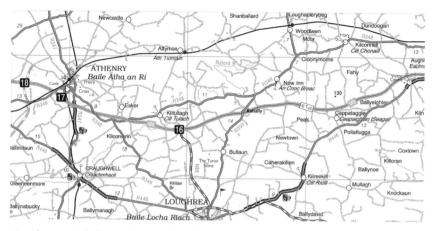

Map showing Rahally in relation to Woodlawn. (Reproduced with permission from Ordnance Survey Ireland)

Post-excavation aerial view of Rahally. (Photograph by Marcus Casey for NRA)

Three human burials, one in the newly discovered ringfort ditch, one in the ringfort annex ditch and one within the annex enclosure were also revealed. Moreover, several artefacts representing all periods of human presence on the site were discovered.

EXCAVATION RESULTS

PREHISTORIC HILLFORT

The earliest evidence for human activity at Rahally was the hillfort. It was identified during an ongoing programme of archaeological testing combined with a topographical survey. This programme was aligned to the concurrent excavation of already identified features. When the results of all these investigations were combined, it became apparent that excavated ditch segments represented only minor parts of a larger monument. The visible outlines could be projected to form large circles extending to the north and south – beyond the road. Four defensive ditches were identified, an outer double ditch and two inner single ditches. From east to west the distance between the outer double ditches was around 450m. The area enclosed by the monument was 14.4ha, of which approximately one third fell inside the remit of the excavations. On the western extremity of the site, the outer double ditch was revealed at either side of an upstanding bank, which was then serving as a townland and field boundary.

Excavations proved the hillfort ditches to be up to 4m in width and 1.5m in depth; the outer and inner ditches being more substantial than the middle ditch. Apart from the townland boundary on the western side of the site, no upstanding evidence of defensive banks remained in situ. However, evidence suggests that banks had once existed, indicated by soil that had slumped into the ditches, particularly on the eastern side. A significant amount of large stone was also

Townland and field boundary to the west of the site of Rahally, showing bank and ditches. (Courtesy of CRDS LTD)

found in the eastern double ditch fills, suggesting some form of bank revetment. Only on the northern extremity of the inner ditch, at the hill base, was any variance in defensive features identified. Here the original excavators had not cut the usual U-shaped ditch but had allowed a natural wet or marshy area as substitute. Two aligned entrances occurred in each outer ditch on the east. Corresponding entrances were found on the western side and also in the middle and inner ditches. But there was no evidence of associated post holes or other entrance features. Excavation of the preserved western bank revealed the greater part of it to be a relatively modern structure. A post-medieval pottery sherd was recovered from the body of the bank, which stratigraphically overlay part of the upper fills of the hillfort's inner double ditch. However, the remnants of an earlier bank were revealed at the base, indicating that a potential prehistoric bank did occur roughly aligned with the current bank. The ancient bank had undergone several reconstructions and repairs during the intervening millennia.

ARTEFACTS AND SAMPLES RECOVERED FROM THE HILLFORT

The most important artefact recovered from the Rahally excavations is probably the copper-alloy brooch fragment dated to the second century AD.[19] This artefact is of a scarce type and is of national, as well as of local, interest. Other artefacts recovered from the hillfort's inner ditch include a damaged Neolithic polished stone axe. This, together with a similar example recovered from non-associated topsoil, may indicate activity at Rahally prior to hillfort construction. Although 44 lithics were recovered from the Rahally excavations, less than 25 per cent of these were found in a hillfort context. However, all of the hillfort ditches are represented, and all the lithic finds within these contexts, with the exception of a possibly intrusive whetstone recovered from the inner double ditch, are likely to be of prehistoric origin. The remaining lithic assemblage, which is of a similar composition and includes chert and flint blades, scrapers, flakes, a broken plano-convex knife and two quartzite hammerstones, was recovered from topsoil or from archaeological features postdating hillfort use. Again, all of these, with the possible exception of the hammerstones, are likely to be prehistoric. A damaged bone pin was also recovered from the outer ditch

Radiocarbon dating shows that all three enclosing features at Rahally are roughly contemporary. A charcoal sample taken from the inner ditch fill has returned a radiocarbon date of 994–27 BC. Likewise, a basal sample from the middle ditch returned a date of 1090–00 BC. A basal sample from the outer double ditch returned a date of 790-520 BC. This evidence is supported by the recovery of Late Bronze Age pottery sherds from the inner, middle and outer double ditches. By far the majority of sherds came from the inner ditch, smaller amounts coming from the middle and outer ones. All the sherds proved to be from flat-bottomed bucket-shaped simple coarse-ware vessels. The assemblage represented seven of these vessels: four were thick-walled and three were thin-walled. This type of vessel is known to be suitable for use as tableware as well as for storage. Sherds from similar flat- bottomed vessels were recovered from excavations at Haughey's Fort, County Armagh,[20] and from a ditched enclosure at Ballyveelish, County Tipperary.[21] Only one Rahally pottery sherd showed evidence of potential decoration in the form of two narrow incised parallel lines 15cm apart. A sherd bearing similar decoration was recovered from Ballyveelish, County Tipperary.[22] Dating evidence from these three sites indicates that they are contemporary with Rahally.[23]

Approximately 50 per cent of the total 5,705 animal bones sampled at Rahally came from a prehistoric context. All four hillfort ditches were represented and by far the majority of animal bone belonged to cattle. No fish bone was found and bird bone was scarce. Antlers proved to have been sourced both from the collection of shed specimen and the killing of deer. In some instances, antler fragments had been used as picks. Bones from the outer double ditches, coming mostly from cattle (mainly skulls, teeth and limb bones) were not as numerous

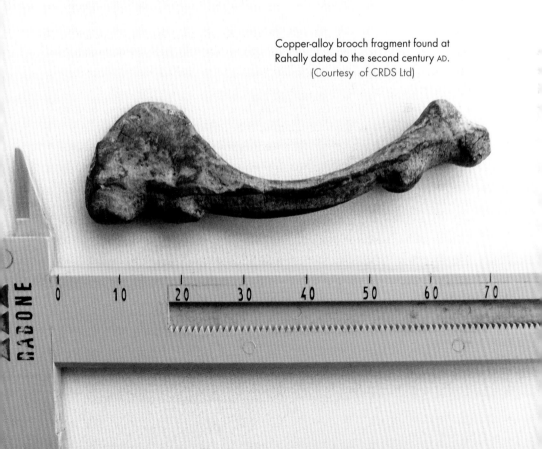

Copper-alloy brooch fragment found at Rahally dated to the second century AD. (Courtesy of CRDS Ltd)

as in other areas. Seven fragments of red-deer antler, one of which was evidently shed, two horse teeth, the radius of a hare and a few pig and sheep bones were among those recovered. Over 1,420 bone specimens were collected from the middle ditch. Cattle were again the most numerous, followed by pig, red deer and sheep. Two corncrake, one duck, nine hare and one probable wildcat bone were included in the collection. Twenty-seven bone specimens proved to be those of a large immature dog with an estimated shoulder height of 62.5cm. All cattle ages were represented, including four calves. Approximately 1,000 bone specimens were recovered from the inner ditch. Again cattle bone was most frequent, followed by red deer, then pig and sheep. Many of the deer had been killed when they were about 2 or 3 years old. Bone from a 2- or 3-week-old piglet bore old cut marks. Two large dogs were represented among the specimens, and there was one plover bone.

HILLFORT DISCUSSION

Hillforts are described by Grogan as 'large hilltop sites defined by substantial ramparts that take advantage of the natural defensive properties of the topography'.[24] It is accepted that Irish hillforts originate in the later half of the second millennium BC, and that construction of this type of monument continued for several centuries at least. The number of identified Irish hillforts has increased over the last half century or so. In 1972, Raftery suggested forty sites, and noted that a 1951 publication on the Irish Iron Age did not even consider hillforts.[25] Some twenty years later, the estimated number of Irish hillforts had increased to between sixty and eighty.[26] Grogan's 2005 study is based on seventy-four known sites. O'Sullivan suggests about ninety sites.[27] Barry Raftery has classified three categories of Irish hillforts, based on the number of defences and height above sea level.[28] The North Munster Project has further refined classification, based on size.[29] Rahally is a Class 2 hillfort, being a multivallate hilltop enclosure exceeding 5ha. Class 2 hillforts are most common in the south and west of the country. Rahally is among the largest found to date in the Class 2 category. At 104m OD, it is not particularly elevated in the landscape, but it does command a view of the countryside, particularly to the north, east and west.

   The function of the hillfort has been the subject of much discussion. Indeed our current knowledge of Irish hillforts is based on a small number of partial excavations at Freestone Hill, Rathgall, Haughey's Fort, Mooghaun and Dun Aonghasa, all of which have been partially excavated to date.[30]

Grogan has identified relevant research questions regarding hillforts.[31] These include the status of hillforts as centres of permanent populations or of high-status families; their periods of occupancy and their role as ritual, industrial and military sites. Addressing Grogan's research questions in reference to Rahally only slightly enhances our chances of a correct interpretation. Approximately 5 per cent of known Irish hillforts have been partially excavated to date. However, bearing in mind that the inner hillfort citadel at Rahally was re-occupied during the early medieval periods, there was no evidence uncovered to suggest that the site had a permanent population in prehistory. Nor was evidence produced to prove that it had been the residence of a high-status family. Rahally could conceivably have been occupied during times of stress. A natural water course ran through the site. But this originated outside the hillfort and could have been diverted if the fort was under siege. Should the hillfort have been the focus of settlement, it is probable that a substantial amount of pottery sherds and lithics would have been found, rather than the sparse collection recovered during the excavation. Seven pottery vessels do not indicate settlement, especially as the majority of these were discovered in the same general location, at the base of the inner ditch. The only other datable artefact from this hillfort context is the copper-alloy brooch fragment, which potentially postdates the pottery sherds by as much as 1,000 years. There was no evidence of permanent occupation during this millennium. Nor was there evidence of serious prehistoric industrial activity at Rahally.

Did hillforts have a military role? Grogan suggests that accessibility probably reflects the function of a hillfort.[32] Unlike other hillforts, such as Ballylin, County Limerick (28:085), Turlough Hill, County Clare (3:036) and Knocknashee, County Sligo (33:013), Rahally might be described as being easily accessible. It is noteworthy that the lithic assemblage recovered during the course of the excavation, either from hillfort-associated contexts or from topsoil in the vicinity, represents the everyday trade and working tools of the period. Scrapers, short blades and sharp flakes are associated more with food and clothing processing than with military matters. No prehistoric weaponry of any kind was recovered during the excavations. The defences at Rahally seem symbolic when compared to some British or continental examples.[33] To defend the outer circumference of Rahally would have involved a large number of people. But in keeping with a hillfort's use of the topography, wet or marshy land occurs to the north and south-east of the site. O'Sullivan has noted that although Rahally is relatively low-lying, it commands a view of the countryside northwards towards the *Slí Mór*, a principal ancient roadway leading to the west coast, and that it also overlooks the meeting point of three baronies – Athenry, Loughrea and Kilconnell.[34] Perhaps if the hillfort did play a military role, this was symbolic, as it was visible from the ancient roadway and also from neighbouring chiefdoms.

In the absence of contradictory evidence, is it likely that Grogan's remaining research question, concerning the ritual role of hillforts, provides the most likely answer when related to Rahally? The discovery of red-deer and large-dog bone suggests the Iron Age culture of the hunt and tales of the Fíanna. It may be also significant that the only prehistoric metal artefact from the site was recovered from a wet context. As it is not uncommon to recover artefacts from such contexts, perhaps its deposition was associated with Iron Age rituals.[35] The excavations at Rahally have not provided any positive evidence to determine the precise use of the site, but perhaps they have, when studied in combination with excavations of similar sites, helped to bring us closer to an overall understanding of Irish hillforts.

EARLY MEDIEVAL PERIOD

RINGFORT

The newly discovered eastern ringfort was univallate and sub-circular in plan, and measured 32m in diameter. An entrance faced south-west, towards the

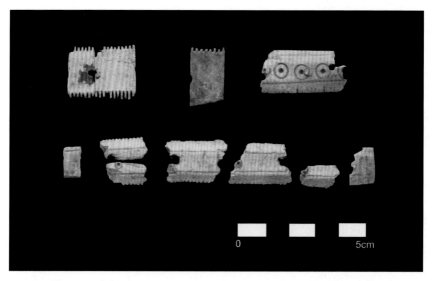

Decorated bone comb fragments. (Photographed by John Sunderland for CRDS Ltd)

larger and potentially higher-status bivallate Rahally ringfort (GA86:211).
A similar relationship between ringforts was found to occur at Lisleagh,
County Cork.[36] The enclosing ditch measured up to 2m in width and 1.25m in
depth, stratigraphically postdating the outer hillfort double ditches. Much of
the interior and the eastern ditch segment had been truncated by agriculture
over the centuries. An interior curvilinear gully was partially preserved;
its location suggests that it served to drain water from an internal bank.
Some similarly located gullies were excavated at Dressogagh Rath, County
Armagh.[37] Four internal pits, likely to be associated with the ringfort's period
of occupancy, were also identified.

ARTEFACTS AND SAMPLES RECOVERED FROM THE RINGFORT DITCH

A charcoal sample from a secondary ditch fill returned a date of AD 680–890.
The ditch also produced interesting finds, including large amounts of cut bone and
antler, two metal blades, and decorated bone-comb fragments. A blue glass bead
and a base-metal finger ring, likely to predate AD 600 (Martin Jones pers. comm.),
were also found in the ditch. A human burial (female aged 36–45 years old) was
recovered from the ditch base. Radiocarbon dating from a bone sample returned

Excavations in the
ringfort annex.

a date of AD 890–1030. There was no indication of a grave cutting and it seems that the body was lodged in the ditch at the time of backfilling.

A large animal-bone assemblage was also collected from the medieval features at Rahally. The newly discovered eastern ringfort ditch produced 1,280 specimens. Cattle were by far the most numerous, followed by red deer, sheep, horse and pig. It was evident from cut marks on a stag bone that the animal had been skinned. Much of the antler, but only one cattle bone, had been worked. Thirty-eight dog bones, representing two dogs that, though large, had been smaller than those from the prehistoric period, were included in the collection. Gnawed cattle bone was also recovered from the ditch, as were two hare bones and one of passerine (bird).

THE ANNEX

The second monument representing the early medieval period at Rahally was an annex, located immediately east of the preserved bivallate ringfort (GA86:211). It was sub-circular in plan and measured approximately 38m by 40m.

The enclosing ditch was comparatively V-shaped, unlike the hillfort ditches. Widths were up to 3m and depths up to 1.2m. A charcoal sample from a secondary ditch fill was dated to AD 1020–1180. Evidence for an internal bank was identified

The annex ditch interior. The white markers show the location of postholes.

on the eastern and western interiors of the ditch. No stratigraphic relationship was discovered between the annex and the preserved ringfort. As the hilltop had previously been the centre of the hillfort, it is not surprising that charcoal from a linear cutting within the ditch returned an Iron Age date (380–180 BC). A burnt pit located east of the enclosure returned a date of 200–40 BC. The southern annex edge extended beyond the road corridor. But a terminus was located just inside the boundary, perhaps indicating an entrance. All archaeological features within the annex were concentrated on the southern side. These include a complex series of linear cuttings, perhaps representing gullies, slot trenches or wall footings. It is possible that at least some of these linear features represent later furrows. A metalled surface, a dumbbell kiln, pits and a series of postholes, semi-circular in plan, extended beyond the limits of the excavation. Two substantial postholes occur in this area, one within the semi-circle and one west of the group. A charcoal sample from the base of the dumbbell kiln has been dated to AD 1215–1285 and a truncated potential posthole, one of those forming the semi-circle, to AD 1440–1640. It is apparent from this dating evidence that activity continued on the hilltop long after the annex ditch was backfilled.

ARTEFACTS AND SAMPLES ASSOCIATED WITH THE RINGFORT ANNEX

In common with other features on the Rahally site, there were few finds, but those recovered were of good quality and datable. Included were an iron arrowhead from subsoil (later medieval), a copper alloy penannular brooch

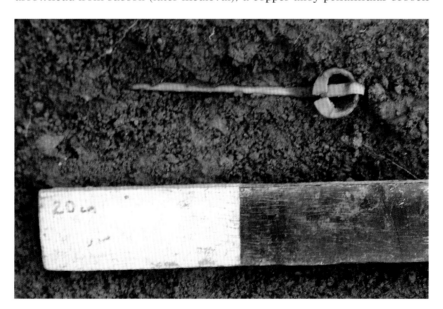

Penannular brooch in situ.

(ninth–tenth century) and a coloured glass bead, both of which came from the upper ditch fill, and some industrial-related worked bone from an internal linear fill. Dating of the artefact types roughly corresponds to the radiocarbon dating of the ditch fill. However, in common with the newly discovered ringfort on the eastern extremity of the site, a partial human child's skeleton was found in the upper fill of the ditch. Radiocarbon dating of a bone sample from these remains has indicated a date of AD 1020–1200. Remnants of a juvenile burial were also found located in subsoil in the northern section of the annex. A bone sample from this individual has been radiocarbon-dated to AD 990–1160. No grave cutting was identified for either burial. It seems, in common with the burial in the eastern ringfort, that the remains were likely placed there about the time of final backfilling.

Animal bone specimens from the annex ditch on the hilltop were not as numerous as those from the eastern ringfort but were of similar proportions. However, far less red deer and no worked antler was found. Some cattle bone showed evidence of foot damage, which might indicate draught cattle, rather than domestic breeds reared for food. Bones belonging to at least four dogs were recovered from the ditch. Two adult and two immature dogs were represented. It is probable that at least one was of the Labrador/Collie type. Shoulder height has been calculated from two limb bones to be 50.9cm and 51.5cm. The occurrence of gnawed and digested bone further indicated the presence of dogs on the site. Seven goose bones were included in the assemblage. It was not possible to determine if these belonged to a wild or a domestic variety. Other features within the annex provided mainly cattle bone. But it was from within this area that the only positively identified goat bone was found.

RINGFORT DISCUSSION

Archaeologists agree that ringforts represent farmsteads.[38] Stout states that there are 45,119 examples in Ireland, 41 per cent of which have been 'positively identified'.[39] But the numbers may have been greater. Many destroyed monuments are being recognised during the course of ongoing surveys or found during archaeological testing in the face of development, as happened at Rahally. Ringforts are often locally known by their Gaelic name, *lios* or *ráth*, a term sometimes incorporated into the townland name. Stout, in his study of the national distribution of ringforts, has noted that south-east Connaught is a high-density area.[40] Rahally is close to a main concentration of ringforts between the towns of Ballinasloe and Loughrea. Interior dimensions vary regionally and examples are recorded between 15.5m and 75m. However, 84 per cent of known sites measure between 20m and 44m in diameter. Univallate ringforts, those with one fosse and internal bank, are by far the most common type. Multivallate ringforts, those with two or the rare three banks, account for approximately 19 per cent of the national total. However, 33 per cent of the 1,104 ringforts recorded in north County Galway are bivallate.[41]

Many ringforts preserve evidence of domestic dwellings. Those in which there is no occupation evidence are said to have functioned as cattle enclosures.[42] Because the annex is located immediately east of the preserved high-status bivallate ringfort, it is presumed that both monuments are contemporary. But, as mentioned above, there is no stratigraphic relationship between them. The outline of two potential rectangular structures can be observed within the preserved bivallate ringfort (GA86: 213). These outlines might represent higher-status dwellings, leaving the annex as an enclosed farmyard. The linear outline of features within the annex may represent animal pens or structures, perhaps for sheep, pigs or calves, or young dairy cows. The absence of postholes within potential wall footings is not unusual in rectangular structures.[43] Fergus Kelly has indicated that there is ample evidence for the penning and housing of domestic animals in the early medieval Irish texts.[44] Other linear features within the annex were interpreted as gullies based on their sloping towards the annex ditch. As with many contemporary enclosures, the interior slope is often away from the cold; in this case it's towards the south.[45] A metalled surface, some small postholes, slot-trenches and pits in the south-western quadrant might represent a sheltered working area.

LATER MEDIEVAL PERIOD

FIELD SYSTEM

Excavations at Rahally facilitated the dating of the recorded field-system banks (GA86:213). A charcoal sample from beneath the central bank returned a radiocarbon date of AD 1043–1218. It was also stratigraphically established that the construction of the central field bank postdated the filling of the ringfort-annex ditch. Approximately 90m of the central bank and 15m of the western bank were located within the road corridor. The preserved remnants of both were approximately 2m wide and up to 0.6m high. No associated artefacts were recovered. Although the western bank was more substantial than the central example, excavation proved that both were similarly constructed. Using a 'dump construction' method, clay was dug from the earth and dumped to form a linear/curvilinear bank. Collapsed stones beside the remnants are interpreted as the remnants of dry-stone walling. Mitchell suggests that such curving enclosing banks were found in outlying areas surrounded by commonage.[46] This type of farming was a Norman introduction, which fits the dating of the banks.

EARLY MODERN PERIOD

CORN-DRYING KILN

The early modern period at Rahally was represented by a stone-lined keyhole-type corn-drying kiln. This was located inside the middle hillfort ditch on the eastern side of the site. The construction was of rough field stone and it was cut into the south-facing slope of a natural hollow. The kiln, including the flu, measured 1.35m in width, 2.15m in length and was 0.8m deep, orientated north-south. Although no evidence of a fire pit was identified, charred material and heat-affected stone were identified. The top of the kiln-bowl structure was level with the ground on the northern side. Gaps within the stone structure of the bowl could have been used to support mats. There was no evidence for collapsed roofing materials; perhaps a removable thatched roof had been used.

The hollow, into which the kiln was cut, measures 20m by 30m. This area had been roughly cobbled and evidence for a low dry-stone enclosing wall was revealed on the eastern side. It is probable that this area represented a yard to allow working convenience. Two large pits east of the kiln might be associated with storage. There is ample evidence for working areas in the vicinity of keyhole kilns.[47] Excavation proved that the cobbles had been overgrown by sod, probably following disuse of the kiln. A worn George II Irish-issue halfpenny from the 1740s was recovered from the sod base, indicating that this area was still open, but not necessarily in use, during the latter half of the eighteenth century. This hollow had been subsequently backfilled.

CONCLUSION

The results of the archaeological excavations at Rahally provide evidence of continued agricultural activities over the centuries. Several stone artefacts, including the Neolithic stone axes, might indicate human presence on the hill prior to hillfort construction during the Late Bronze Age. Iron Age presence is indicated by the finding of the rare copper-alloy artefact. The early medieval period is represented by the ringforts. These are followed by a late medieval field system. Radiocarbon dating has shown that there was activity, perhaps even occupation, on the hilltop into the sixteenth century. Agricultural practices are again represented from the seventeenth century to the twentieth, by 'paning and burning', cultivation furrows, a drying kiln and modern field remodelling. Cattle and sheep still occupied the fields at Rahally during the early days of our excavations.

ACKNOWLEDGMENTS

Excavations at Rahally were funded by the National Roads Authority and Galway County Council.

I wish to thank Jerry O'Sullivan and Martin Jones of the National Roads Authority for their support and advice throughout the testing and excavations at Rahally. Fin O'Carroll of Cultural Resources Development Services and the CRDS management team could not have been more helpful during the course of the work.

3

KILLAAN: A DISCUSSION OF THE HISTORY, ARCHAEOLOGY AND TRADITIONS ASSOCIATED WITH THE MEDIEVAL PARISH CHURCH

DR CHRISTY CUNNIFFE

The name Killaan derives from the Gaelic *Cill Leabhainn*, meaning the Church of Leabhainn, or Laan. There are a number of spellings for this name: Laebhan, Leban, Liban, Loebhain, Leaain, to name but a few. Larkin's map of Galway (1817) has the townland spelling as Killean, with the 'Church in Ruins' even at that time. On the Down Survey map (1641) it is rendered as 'Killahan', and located east of 'Moate'.

A reference in the *Annals of the Four Masters* under the year AD 448 informs us that St Laebhan, the person after which this parish is named, was a smith to St Patrick.[48] William Reeves notes that in 'the recital of St. Patrick's *muintir*, or family, ... there occur the names of three smiths (*ghobainn*) expert at shaping, MacCecht, Laebhan, and Fortchern'.[49] The Ordnance Survey Letters for County Galway (1839) discuss Maccectus of Domhnach Loebain, the latter being the parish church in the Diocese of Clonfert, which is Kill-Loebhan, or Killaan today.[50] Maccectus (of Domhnach Loebain) reportedly made the famous relic or shrine called the *finnfaidheach*. If this is the case, then clearly two of Patrick's smiths are associated with the site: Leabhainn, after which the place is named, and MacCecht or Maccectus, who, it is reputed, made the *finnfaidheach*. O'Donovan notes that the relic has been lost through time, and even in the mid-nineteenth century there was no definite idea of what

Excavation of the stone-lined keyhole-type corn drying kiln.

it was. He states that he had 'never met any authority to prove what the *finnfaidheach* was, whether bell, effigy, crosier, mitre, or paten'. He observes that 'Mr. Petrie thinks it was a bell, but he has no evidence to that it was not an effigy'. He argues that 'the bells [of Patrick's age] were of brass or bronze, but as Mac Cechtus was an iron smith (*Faber ferrarius*) the *finnfaidheach* Phadraig was an iron thing and consequently not a bell'.[51] This argument we now know was ill-founded, as St Patrick's bell (preserved in The National Museum of Ireland) is in fact made of iron. Reeves noted that the '*Fionn Faoideach*' was made by MacCecht of Domnanch Laebain.[52] Margaret Stokes, when discussing it, claimed that the 'iron bell of St. Patrick is at once the most authentic and the oldest Irish relic of Christian metal-work that has descended to us. It possesses the singular merit of having an unbroken history through 1400 years'.[53] Lucas further notes that the bell known as the *Clog na Edachla* or the Bell of the Testaments is said to have been in the saint's tomb when it was opened in 553 by St Columba, and that it is mentioned on a number of occasions in the annals over succeeding centuries.[54] More recently, in relation to St Leabhainn in his *Dictionary of Irish Saints*, Pádraig Ó Riain refers to this relic as 'St Patrick's sweet-sounding bell'.[55] Ó Riain also points out that Leabhainn, and Foirthcearn, another of the three smiths, shared the Church of Ballyovey in the barony of Carra, County Mayo.

KILLAAN MEDIEVAL PARISH CHURCH

Killaan, like the bulk of medieval parish churches in the Diocese of Clonfert, has been the object of very little historical research in the past. It would appear on initial investigation that there is a scarcity of documentary material for the place, but with careful reading of the available sources it is possible to develop a fairly decent picture of its history. On investigation of these sources, a number of significant things come to light. First of all, we find that the church is referred to in O'Donovan's letters as '*Domnach-Loebhain*'.[56] The Domnach element of the name provides a clue as to a date of construction of the initial church that stood on the site. Dónall Mac Giolla Easpaig points out that the word Domnach 'is a borrowing of Latin *dominicum*, a word which had a specialised meaning of "church building" in pre fifth-century continental Latin'. He goes on to demonstrate that in an Irish context, it denotes church sites with their origin in the Patrician era (time of St Patrick), and outlines that in many cases it predates the actual churches with which it is now associated. This is the situation with Killaan. The Domnach element (which was the previous prefix) has become displaced by the term Kill, which we find used in conjunction with the personal name Liabhain, anglicised as Killaan. Both elements refer directly to a church site. According to Mac Giolla Easpaig the 'majority of identifiable native saints represented in the "cill" names belong to the sixth and seventh centuries'.[57] This suggests that the church here at Killaan had changed its designation quite early in its history, perhaps within a century or so of its initial foundation.

Killaan is recorded in the 1302–7 taxation list as the rectory of Kiltullagh and Kildagan. It is also noted in the same document as an independent vicarage, under the designation of Kildagan i.e. Killaan.[58] In that taxation list, the rectory is valued jointly with Kiltullagh at 19 marks, providing a tithe of 25*s* 4*d*. The vicarage on the other hand is recorded as having a value of 31*s* 8*d*, returning a tithe of 2*s* 2*d*. This is one of the earliest lists of parish churches available to us. It shows that Killaan has functioned as a parish from the very outset of parish formation in the diocese in the thirteenth century. According to Kenneth Nicholls, the Rectory of Mayn(m)uach (Maenmoy), mentioned in 1446 as being in the possession of Kilcreevanty Convent in the Diocese of Tuam, equates to Kiltullagh and Kildagan noted in the earlier taxation list.[59] A further brief reference is noted by Nicholls in, 'The Visitations of the Diocese of Clonfert, Tuam and Kilmacduagh, *c.*1565–67'.[60] This informs us that Thomas Broagayn was the Vicar of (Kylleayn) Killaan, and notes it as a rectory attached to the convent of Killcreevanty in the Diocese of Tuam, at that time. However, Killaan is clearly situated in the Diocese of Clonfert, so unless it was included among the possessions of one of the convents given over to Kilcreevanty in 1320, this designation is difficult to explain. If that were the case, it would intimate that it had a female house or at least was providing an income to some nearby house of Arrosian nuns. A place known as *Cluain na Chailín*, mentioned as the site of an old church in the Schools Folklore Collection (1937–939) may be a possible candidate, though this is merely conjectural and requires further research.[61] Cloonacalleen townland is within the north-east extremity of the parish, adjacent to Cloonacallis (townland of the chalice). Annette Kehnel cites an entry in the Papal Records for 1435 which records that John Ua Dubhagáin (O'Doogan), a monk in Athlone, was claiming the rectory of Killaan ... belonging to the Diocese of Clonfert.[62] Another papal bull, dated 1451, refers to correspondence between the office of Pope Nicholas V and the bishop and official of Elphin and Cornelius Oscyngyn, a canon of Elphin, mandating them to collate and assign to Cornelius Ocassayn the position of perpetual vicar of the parish church of Kyllaedaynn (Killaan) in the Diocese of Clonfert.[63] This vacancy arose because Breasal O'Kelly, who previously held the position, entered the Augustinian Priory of St Mary, at Gallen, near Ferbane, County Offaly. Cornelieus had previously been dispensed by papal authority, on account of illegitimacy as the son of unmarried parents, and was promoted to holy

The remains of the medieval church at Killaan.

orders and provided with the cure of the said vicarage. However, it appears
from the bull that he was apprehensive about taking up the position due to
the illegal presence of Charles O'Madden and Donatus O'Kelly, both clerks of
the Diocese of Clonfert. Neither O'Kelly nor O'Madden were in possession of
Killaan, but falsely alleged that the canonry and prebend lawfully belonged
to them, making it very difficult for Oscyngyn to take possession. It is also
noted in the same document that the vicarage was valued at 2 marks at that
time. A further papal bull, dated 10 August 1493,[64] was issued when the
pope learned that a 'canonry of the church of Clonfert and the prebend of
Braudmor in the same and the perpetual vicarage of the parish church of
Kyllayn' was vacant, and that it had been for so long that it had devolved back
to the apostolic see. It appears that a John Okeallyd, and a Thady Odubayn,
bearing themselves as priests, had 'detained the canonry and prebend and
the vicarage respectively without any title or support of law ... for a certain
time'. A petition made by William O'Kelly asked the pope to unite the vicarage
to the canonry and prebend and assign it to him for his lifetime. The pope
instructed a man named Eugene to summon:

> John Okeallyd and Thady and others concerned [and if] he finds the canonry
> and prebend and the vicarage to be vacant, ... and if, through diligent
> examination ... he finds William to be suitable, to collate and assign the
> canonry and prebend, ... with plenitude of canon law, to William and unite

Octagonal cross-shaft re-used as grave
marker in Killaan graveyard.

the vicarage, whose annual value also does not exceed 3 marks sterling, thereto, with all rights and appurtenances, for his lifetime.

Eugene was ordered, if having found in favour of William, to remove John Okeallyd from the canonry and prebend, and Thady from the vicarage and to remove any other unlawful detainers, and to promote William (or his proctor) as a canon of the Church of Clonfert. The pope further instructed that, on the death or resignation of William O'Kelly, the union should be dissolved and the vicarage revert to its original condition and therefore be deemed vacant. What is evident from these couple of bulls is that O'Kelly and O'Doogan appear to be the dominant names associated with the life of this church during the fifteenth century.

The church ruin that stands here today has a well defined external base batter to its north wall, but due to its poor state of preservation bears no other defining features. Its windows and doors, the features most frequently used by architectural historians to date buildings of this nature, are lost. All that remains is one corner of the building. However, a study of the crude stone grave-markers in the surrounding graveyard found a few examples that bear traces of diagonal tooling typical of a late twelfth- or early thirteenth-century date. The existence of these and the presence of the base batter suggest that this church was probably built in the early thirteenth century. An octagonal holy-water font or stoup alleged to have originated from here bears diagonal tooling, so is also likely to have derived from the original phase of the current medieval church. It has been incorporated into a modern gate pier in the new section of the graveyard. This date is in keeping with the establishment of a structured parish system in the Diocese of Clonfert. A few fragments of masonry of late medieval date are to be seen in the graveyard. Their survival allows us to speculate with some authority that the church underwent a further phase of building in the late medieval period. It was quite common for churches to be modified in the fifteenth century. A quick tour of the diocese shows evidence for the enlargement and embellishment of several parish churches at this time.[65] Evidence of religious activity on the site during the seventeenth century is derived from the presence of a section of an octagonal cross-shaft from that time, now reused as a modern grave-marker. It is likely that the Franciscan friars resident at nearby Kilconnell Abbey were active in the wider hinterland, perhaps preaching at this late cross. This was at a time when, despite the oppressive Penal Laws, signs of Catholic revival were apparent in the diocese. It is not known if the church itself was still in use at this stage, but it is possible that religious gatherings still occurred here. This singular fragment is similar in appearance and general profile to two sections of a cross found nearby at Grange, and to the fully intact preaching cross erected in the centre of Kilconnell Village. All three church sites are situated in close proximity. Taking the Kilconnell cross as the key example, we can postulate that these other two crosses were similar in design when in use; consisting of a composite calvary base and an octagonal shaft with an expanded collar, usually bearing a dedicatory inscription and an upper cross rising from the collar. Crosses in graveyards in Clonfert Diocese were more common than generally thought. An unpublished survey undertaken by the writer has highlighted the remains of upwards of twelve surviving examples.

Richard Hayman makes the point that it is 'always worth looking beyond the boundaries of the churchyard for clues as to why churches were built in particular places'.[66] The setting chosen for Killaan church is by no means accidental. First of all, it appears to have had a pre-Christian presence in the landscape as a Lughnasa site (where the season of Harvest was celebrated). Secondly, it is situated at a point where a number of eskers and sand hills converge, thus at the nucleus of several potential medieval communication routes. Our overall knowledge of road systems in the prehistoric and medieval period is quite poor. A number of scholars have attempted to deal with this matter, among them Colm Ó Lochlainn and Linda Doran.[67] A book based on a television series by German scholar Hermann Geissel traced the route of the *Slí Mhór* across the country through Clonmacnoise to Clarenbridge, and noted that it followed the Esker Riada. The author documents the route as passing by the site at Killaan.[68] Like O'Donovan and Ó Lochlainn, he was happy to accept this as its original route. Also of importance to our understanding of how the economy of the parish church functioned is the presence of an area of ground designated as glebe lands immediately south of the church and graveyard. Its proximity to the church shows it to be originally the glebe associated with this site. Glebe lands were critical for the upkeep of the incumbent priest. An entry in the *Books of Survey and Distribution* informs us that a Laughlin Kilpatrick, William Morris and Thomas Morris held 15 acres of glebe land in equal shares between them in the seventeenth century.[69]

Additional to the presence of the church, evidence of secular settlement is also clearly discernible in the wider landscape. This is demonstrated by the survival of a large number of well-preserved ringforts. This particular monument type represents the dispersed settlements of the medieval farmers. Early Christian church settlements tended to be located on the periphery of large populations. An enclosure (GA086-15001) recorded immediately to the south of the present graveyard in the townland of Woodlawn (formerly Moate) was possibly a ringfort. Its relationship, if any, to the church, cannot be established at this point in time, but its proximity would seem to suggest that there was a connection.

Killaan functioned as a parish church from the outset of parish formation in the thirteenth century as can be attested from the 1302 taxation list. What is more difficult to determine from the surviving archaeology is when exactly it was founded. A simple methodology devised by Leo Swan and refined by Etienne Rynne proposes that an early Christian ecclesiastical site can be identified by the presence of any three of about fourteen different elements.[70] When we examine Killaan, we find that five of these constituent elements are present, thus qualifying it as early Christian in origin. It has an associated saint's name, a designated patron day, a holy well, a medieval church, a graveyard and a bullaun stone that is also likely to be related to the site.

On the weight of evidence, both archaeological and historical, it is obvious that Killaan can be acknowledged as early Christian in origin. Nevertheless, some obvious features are absent; there is no evidence of an early Christian cross-inscribed slab, nor is there any indication of there ever having been a round tower or high cross on the site. In fact there are only two sites in Clonfert Diocese where cross slabs are found. One is located at Clonfert (the cathedral centre) and the other in a little-known graveyard, named Gortaganny near the shores of Lough Derg. Interestingly no high cross and only one round tower have been identified in the diocese. This is at Kilmeen, an island parish belonging to the Diocese of Tuam. Therefore, their absence here should be of no great surprise.

ST LAAN'S WELL AND PATTERN

Two holy wells are recorded for Killaan by the Archaeological Survey of Ireland: Tobair Laan (GA086-149) and St Killaan's Well (GA086-150). Both of the wells, as can be deduced from their designations, are dedicated to St Leabhain or Laan. However, only one well, Tobair Laan, is marked on the first-edition OS map causing considerable confusion for the historian.

St Killaan's Well is depicted for the first time on the 1926 revised 6 inch sheet, and is difficult to explain. O'Donovan clearly refers to a pattern at Tobair Laan. Both the entry in the *Archaeological Inventory for County Galway* Vol. II and the results of fieldwork by the writer concur that the well known as St Killaan's Well is the one most likely to have been associated with the annual pattern.[71] It is the well closest to the church and consists of the poorly preserved remains of a roughly circular hollow set within a low rectangular dry-stone enclosure (N-S 3.5m, E-W 2.65). Attached to the east of this is a similar rectangular structure (N-S 4.8m, E-W 2.95m). Both structures are constructed of partially moss-covered limestone blocks, standing to a maximum of 50cm high with outer stones set erect. The most easterly structure is quite overgrown by nettles and the southern wall is 1.6cm thick, while the northern wall is only 90cm thick. A small stand of blackthorn encompasses the site. Due to a change in the local hydrology the well is generally dry, but when the water table is high it fills up with water.

No votive offerings were discernible at the time the well was surveyed by the archaeological survey team in the 1980s. However, a number of small pieces of quartz noted by the writer during recent investigations may well be votive in nature. Deposits of quartz pebbles are a feature commonly associated with holy wells. This particular well is not illustrated on the first-edition OS map (1839). As it is called St Killaan's Well, it too is dedicated to St Laan. It is uncertain when it first came into being. It is strange that two wells in close proximity should be dedicated to the same saint. While it seems implausible that it should have been confused or overlooked at the time of the Ordnance Survey, it seems equally amazing that it could be of late nineteenth- or early twentieth-century origin, and for this not be remembered in local folk tradition. Perhaps we should be alarmed by O'Donovan's own comment when he writes about Killaan. He states, 'I am just sick of church yards, skulls and mouldering walls of churches and the misery of it'.[72] He was obviously becoming weary due to the heavy workload and thus could easily have made mistakes. At this point

St Killaan's Well. (Recorded Monument GA086:150(3))

in time, archaeological excavation is probably the only means of resolving this issue. Located in a field to the north-east of this is 'Tobair Laan', or St Laan's Well. This well is marked on the first-edition OS map. During the archaeological survey carried out in 1985, the well was described as 'D'-shaped in ground plan and surrounded by a line of drystone walling reaching an average height of 15cm. A modern iron railing is built on the top of the wall.[73] A stream clearly visible beside the well on the 1840s map has become overgrown and is now barely discernible in the landscape. A shore that linked the well to the stream is identified by the presence of a box-like opening in the enclosing wall. Local information recalls its use as a domestic well. The water is made accessible by a series of steps.

John O'Donovan stated in his letters, 'there is a holy well near the old church called *Tobair Leadhain* at which a "pattern" was held on Garland Sunday (*Domhnach na b-fear* or *Chroim Duibh*) in honour of St Laan, the patron of the parish'.[74] Garland Sunday, or Fraughan Sunday as it is also known in many places, is the last Sunday in July, and is traditionally a day of veneration at holy wells. Garland Sunday originated as an important pagan festival of the harvest known as *Lughnasa*. Maura Mc Neill in her seminal work on the subject, *The Festival of Lughnasa*, refers briefly to the celebrations at Tobar Laan.[75] It seems evident from the available information that this holy well formed a part in some sort of pre-Christian celebration here at Killaan and therefore it is perhaps the oldest surviving element on the site. Many early Christian ecclesiastical sites had a pagan origin. Early Christian missioners were keen to convert these sites to the new religion, but they rarely managed to completely destroy the rituals associated with the older faith. As late as the 1930s it was still remembered that an annual gathering or patron day took place here. In its original form it is likely to have included a fair of sorts, games, music, drinking, intermixed with the practice of popular religious devotion at the well. A short entry recorded in the School Folklore Collection from Woodlawn School supports this, and relates that, 'there is the remains of a holy well near Killaan graveyard.[76] Every year in the month of July people came here to do Stations. Always at the Stations the people began to argue so on account of that there was a stop put to them'. This appears to be a subtle reference to the banning of the annual pattern by the church. Many patterns were forbidden due to the levels of alcohol consumed, the faction fights that ensued and general immoral behaviour that took place at them.

The holy wells discussed above are in close proximity to the church and form part of the greater religious complex. A bullaun stone (GA086-148) is also recorded for the townland. While it is on the edge of the townland it may have been originally associated with the early Christian settlement.

4

'A SEAT IMPROVED ENTIRELY IN THE MODERN ENGLISH TASTE': THE HISTORY OF THE WOODLAWN ESTATE 1750–1850[77]

BRÍD MERCER

Woodlawn House is a large Victorian mansion located just north-west of the village of New Inn in East Galway. Until recently it was screened from public view by a dense conifer plantation, but this has now been harvested and the house is currently visible from the nearby R348, where, from a distance, it is an impressive sight. Unfortunately, closer inspection reveals the peeling paint, boarded-up windows, ruined outbuildings and the ravaged and fenced-off parkland. Woodlawn, once one of Ireland's largest and richest estates, was founded at the beginning of the eighteenth century by John Trench, the Dean of Raphoe, and remained in Trench family ownership until the mid-1940s.

In 1702, John Trench, a high-ranking Anglican clergyman, bought the land around Woodlawn (still known by its Irish name Moate) from the Government. The land had been confiscated by the Crown from the Jacobite Peter Martin after the war between King William III and King James. Dean Trench continued to live in Raphoe, County Donegal but later moved to Dublin where he died in 1725.[78] The land then passed to his son Frederick, a Dublin lawyer who had previously married the wealthy heiress Mary Geering. In 1731 Frederick was one of the first members of the newly established Royal Dublin Society,[79] the aims of which were to promote new ideas about agriculture and estate management.

Another early member of the RDS was Sir James Caldwell of Castle Caldwell in Fermanagh and in 1750 Frederick wrote inviting him to Mote [*sic*] in 1750.[80] In 1754 Frederick's oldest son, also called Frederick, born in 1722, married the heiress Mary Sadleir of Sopwell Hall in Tipperary.[81] Her marriage settlement for £5,000 shows how wealthy the Trenches had now become, because as well as several thousand acres at Moate, it gives extensive land holdings in King's County (Offaly) as well as property in Dublin.[82] In February of 1758[83] Frederick Trench the elder and his wife Mary died within a week of each other and after this, the young couple commenced building on their Galway lands.

Their newly built house was called 'Woodlawn', perhaps reflecting Frederick's ambitions for the creation of an ersatz English pastoral landscape. It must have been renamed before 1763, as Frederick Trench wrote to his first cousin Sir James Caldwell then from Woodlawn thanking him for his offer to send fruit trees, but saying not to bother, as his garden walls were already full. This work must have eaten into Frederick's capital as he bemoans the lack of ready money in his letter: 'I need not tell you I have none'.[84] Much of this money must have been used up in the extensive bog-drainage projects carried out by Frederick around this time. These were such a success that over fifty years later they were being held up as a model by a parliamentary commission on land improvement.[85] The wish to improve was not confined to the land; progressive landlords like Frederick Trench believed in educating their tenants and in 1770 he applied for a grant to the Royal Dublin Society to construct a school in Woodlawn.[86] Royal Dublin Society schools were intended to convert the poor to Protestantism as well as to educate and may have provoked the opposition of the local Catholic clergy. In the next century, an inspection of Woodlawn National School notes tersely that the Roman Catholic clergyman 'does not attend'.[87]

Woodlawn House, entrance front, from south. (Courtesy of Anne Carey)

In 1776 Frederick's efforts at Woodlawn were crowned with a visit by Arthur
Young, the noted English agriculturist who visited Woodlawn on his tour of
Ireland.[88] Young had heard of Frederick's bog-reclamation schemes and he happily
escorted him around the estate: 'nobody could be more anxious to have me in
general well informed'. Young noted with approval: 'Woodlawn is a seat improved
entirely in the modern English taste, and is as advantageous a copy of it as I have
anywhere seen. The house stands on the brow of a trifling ground, which looks
over a lawn dwelling into gentle inequalities ...' Several years after the death of
Frederick Trench, another visitor wrote in 1808: 'Woodlawn is beautiful ... this
mansion is splendidly and elegantly furnished, and the interior and exterior...,
evinced his [Lord Ashtown's] predecessor's good taste, by whom it was built'.[89]

Woodlawn House appears in a thumbnail sketch in Taylor and Skinner's
Roadmaps of Ireland published in 1776 showing a house with main block and
two single-storey wings set in wooded landscape; the layout of the grounds
appears in more detail in William Larkin's 1819 map of Galway and later in
the first-edition Ordnance Survey in 1838.

Both of these maps show a tripartite house facing a serpentine lake set in
carefully designed parkland. Here sinuous belts of trees are separated by avenues,
and lawns and water features show the influence of fashionable English gardeners
like Capability Brown of whom it was said: 'His style of smooth undulating

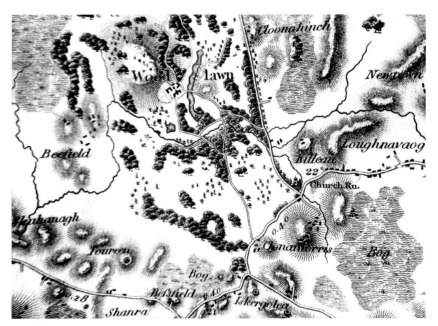

Section of William Larkin's 1819 Map of Galway. (Photograph taken by B. Doherty, courtesy
of the National Library of Ireland)

The Trench Mausoleum. (Photograph taken by Ms Sheila Counihan)

grass ... clumps, belts and scattering of trees and his serpentine lakes ..., forms a "gardenless" form of landscape gardening'.[90] There is unfortunately very little trace left of this parkland as it disappeared under later conifer plantations.

Another structure from around this time is the family mausoleum which lies on a hill a mile or so north-east of the house. It is a stone-built concentric structure with a central tower approximately 40 feet high surrounded by a lawned area approximately 100 feet in diameter encircled by a 12 feet high castellated curtain wall. The architectural historian Maurice Craig says that: 'it is the largest (in area) private mausoleum in Ireland'.[91] Frederick Trench and his wife Mary are buried in the table tomb in the tower and his descendants are buried in the enclosed lawn surrounding the tower.

One of the most prominent graves belongs to the 1st Lord Ashtown. He was the oldest son of Frederick Trench, born in Dublin in 1755, and, after the family custom, called Frederick like his father. In 1785 he married Elizabeth Robinson but the couple had no children. He was the MP for the borough of Portarlington in the Irish House of Commons between 1798 and the Act of Union in 1801. After this he was created Baron Ashtown of Moate in the Peerage of Ireland on 27 December 1800, just four days before the Act of Union came into force on 1 January 1801. This coincidence has lead to accusations that the title was a Union peerage, that is, it had been granted in exchange for Frederick Trench's vote for the Union. This was indignantly denied in the Cooke-Trench memoir published later in the century[92] and Frederick Trench had previously indicated his support for the Union in an open letter to the *Freeman's Journal* in 1798, the year before the crucial vote.[93] The peerage was probably a reward for Frederick Trench's longstanding political support for the Union, not the price of a single vote.

The official title given to Frederick Trench for his support was 'Baron Ashtown of Moate'; 'Moate' refers to the original Irish name for Woodlawn, but the origin of 'Ashtown' is less clear. Samuel Lewis writing in 1837 says that: 'A village in this parish called in Irish Bollin Whin Souge or "Ash Village" gives the title of Baron to Lord Ashtown';[94] but there is no townland of the name in the area. It is more likely that the title brings in a reference to Dublin because the Trenches had extensive property there, particularly in the suburb of Ashtown. It is unusual as it descends not to the heirs of the 1st Lord Ashtown (who was childless), but to the male heirs of his father, Frederick Trench of Woodlawn, in what is known as a special remainder. Since Frederick's six younger sons have many living male descendants, it is unlikely that the title will die out. Because of the special remainder, the 1st Lord Ashtown was succeeded by his nephew, the 2nd Lord Ashtown, the oldest son of his brother Francis, from whom the 7th Lord Ashtown, Sir Nigel Clive Trench KCMG, the former UK ambassador to Korea and Portugal, who died on 6 March 2010 (RIP), was also descended. He was laid to rest in the mausoleum on 16 May 2010 and was succeeded by his son, the 8th Lord Ashtown, Roderick Nigel Godolphin Trench.

The Ashtowns were a cadet branch of the Earls of Clancarty in Ballinasloe (Frederick of Garbally's descendants) and part of a network of Trench cousins around Ireland. Henry Inglis, on his tour of Ireland, visited Ballinasloe in 1834 and met:

> Lord Clancarty, the head of the Trench family, who are, I may say, a race, and that a numerous one of improvers. I never passed through Ireland where I found one of the name located, that I did not see their demesnes well ordered, their farming well managed, and a benevolent and prudent attention paid to the education, the comforts, and as far as they were allowed, the religious instruction of the lower classes.[95]

There was no shortage of candidates in the family to supply the vacancy the 1st Lord Ashtown left when he moved to England a few years after he had been granted the title. When he was named as an absentee landlord, a friend rallied to his defence:

In some instances his [Wakefield's] information is not accurate, as when he says Lord Ashtown is an Absentee – altho' he lives half the year, with great hospitality at Woodlawn, farms a considerable extent of Ground, with all modern English improvements, has greatly embellished his paternal mansion & the grounds around it – has bettered the condition of the Laborer by paying him in money …[96]

Lord and Lady Ashtown lived at Chessel House in Hampshire but frequently visited Bath and other fashionable spa towns. After his death in Bath in 1840, Lord Ashtown was buried in the mausoleum on the family estate in Woodlawn, together with his wife Elizabeth who died in 1844. While the 1st Lord Ashtown lived in England, it was John Trench, his youngest brother, who managed the estate in his absence between 1800 and 1838 until the coming of age of his nephew Frederick Mason Trench, who had been brought up on the Sopwell Hall Estate in County Tipperary. During this time, John Trench took an active part in public life: he was a magistrate, a commissioner for stamps, served on the Galway Grand Jury as well as being manager of the local school (the road to which was described as 'swarming with children at play')[97] and farmed on his own account. In 1839 he was made a life member of the Royal Dublin Society in recognition of his contribution to agriculture. When Frederick Mason Trench inherited the estate in 1840, John Trench retired to his house at St Catherine's Park, Leixlip County Kildare and was buried in the mausoleum at Woodlawn in 1858.

In 1819 John Trench had been a witness to the Bog Commissioners, which praised the bog-reclamation schemes his father Frederick started in 1760. These ranged over 232 English acres and were held up as a model of good practice for other estates.[98] Later in 1836 he was also a witness to the Commission into the Condition of the Poorer Classes in Ireland. In this he says that labourers on the estate 'were employed all the year at 6d a day … the condition of the men … distinguished by the better houses, better clothes and all being in possession of a cow'.[99] But a different picture of the area emerges in the testimony of Dr Harrison, the dispensary doctor in Killane, given to the same Commission. Dr Harrison lived in the dispensary premises (located beside Woodlawn Church of Ireland) established in 1822, and his salary was 90s per year. He treated approximately 1,000 people per year; the principal diseases being pulmonary diseases and rheumatism.

The population is wholly agricultural and very numerous; their clothing tolerable; food very bad and deficient in quantity in bad seasons; bedding in general bad; furniture little or none; ventilation extremely bad. In answer to the question: Have you experienced many instances where actual disease has been brought on by lack of sustenance ... ? he replied flatly I have, many instances. And in answer to Have you found any particular type of food promotive of disease among the poorer classes? he answered: Bad potatoes: which is the only food in use among the poorer class.[100]

Some of the doctor's patients may have come from other estates in the area, but it is an indication of how hard life was for the rural poor even on a well run estate. It got even harder when the potato crop failed. One of the worse failures before the Great Famine occurred in 1826 and a letter sent by Lord Ashtown to the Chief Secretary in 1826 requesting help from the Government states that 'my brother John and his wife have set up a soup kitchen in the house [Woodlawn] and helped up to 600 people and are obliged to send some away'.[101]

The Commission also asked doctors about the use of strong spirits amongst the poor. However, unlike in other areas, Dr Harrison reported that the use of strong spirits around Woodlawn was 'not prevalent'.[102] Perhaps this was due to the religious influence of John and his wife Jean Trench who set up a Sunday school in the mansion house, a past pupil of whom was Thomas McCullagh, a celebrated Methodist minister; he spoke of them as 'a godly family who care for the material and spiritual health of their neighbours'.[103] There had always been a strong religious influence in the family from the beginning; the extended family included many high-ranking Church of Ireland clergy, such as the Archbishop of Dublin Richard Chenevix Trench. The 1st Lord Ashtown himself set up a branch of the Bible Society in Southampton whose aim was to purchase and distribute Bibles to the poor for missionary purposes (including Ireland). This was a venture unlikely to have met the approval of the Catholic Church. Later in 1863 there was friction between Protestants and Catholics when the stationmaster at Woodlawn Mr Smith died. His funeral turned into a riot as both Catholic and Protestant ministers read the funeral service over the dead man.[104] But the 1st Lord Ashtown and his brother John believed in the need to end the discrimination that Catholics faced in entering public life. Both signed open letters to the Government in 1826 requesting Catholic emancipation and both contributed to the erection of a Catholic church in Kilconnell in 1838.[105]

After the 1st Lord Ashtown died in England, his nephew Frederick Mason Trench inherited the extensive family estates in Tipperary, Offaly, Dublin and Galway. But he only succeeded to the title after an inquisition by the House of Lords in 1855. This inquisition drew heavily on the evidence from the family

Bible, which dates back to the earlier eighteenth century (and is still in the family).[106] The 2nd Lord Ashtown married Harriette Cosby of Stradbally Hall in County Laois in 1831 and they had four children. The couple moved to Woodlawn around the death of the 1st Lord Ashtown in 1840 and Frederick Mason Trench became deputy lieutenant for County Galway the same year as well as sitting as a magistrate. Lady Ashtown died at the age of 34 in 1845 and was buried in the mausoleum. Her obituary stated that at her funeral 'such a manifestation of love and esteem for an individual has never before been evinced ... in the neighbourhood'.[107]

In 1846 the potato failed and the Great Famine struck, decimating the population of the Irish countryside until 1849. The cash books of the Woodlawn estate are in the National Library of Ireland: the earliest of these dates from 1849 and lists only ten tenants on the Woodlawn estate with a total rental of £312 6s 10d, whereas several years later the rental for Woodlawn is over £2,000.[108] There are several references to payments to the schoolmaster, R.L. Foreman: 'a cheque ... being to pay labour ... on the Woodlawn Estate, one for the substantial amount of £60'. The ledger also records a payment to the schoolmaster at Brackna for *labour* during this period. Were these Famine relief works? One clue that they might be comes in 1852 when there is an entry recording a payment of £5 to Mr Foreman 'for paying men for the last two years'. Less sympathetically, there is also a payment in 1850 for 'costs of ejectment'. Evidence given to the Congested Districts Board in 1906 claimed that there had been many evictions on the Woodlawn estate during the Famine,[109] but this is not supported in local folk memory and it is unlikely that mass evictions would have been forgotten or forgiven.

Undoubtedly the population of the estate fell, whether through eviction, emigration or death, as it did all over Ireland. Local clergymen wrote to the Famine Relief Commissioners in Dublin stating the urgency of the situation. The parish priest of Ballymacward, Fr Derry (later Bishop of Clonfert), writing in 1846 spoke of hundreds of poor families in danger of starvation and said that, apart from a few exceptions, the local gentry had done very little to help the poor.[110] The Anglican vicar at Kilconnell, the Revd Robert Collis, writing in August 1846 described the 'almost total failure of the potato crop ... the potato tops are black and withered around the whole neighbourhood'. His letter also observed that a small number of tenants in the parish had all the best pasture land with only a few herds (cattlemen) to manage the stock, and the rest of the population crammed onto the poorer land.[111]

This would help to explain anomalies in the population census returns published in 1851, which show the effects of the Famine on the locality.[112]

In this, some townlands show no change in population, a small drop or even an increase. Other townlands show a huge drop in population. A random selection of townlands on the estate is given in the below table. More detailed analysis of this data is required to establish whether the townlands with the greatest falls in population were those on the poorer lands on the estate, but a cursory glance at the Poor Law valuations and acreages supports that conclusion.

Townland	Population in 1841	Population in 1851	% increase or decrease
Woodlawn	39	52	+33.3
Tullawicky	77	33	- 57.0
Greenhills	33	30	-9.9
Moneyveen	85	6	-92.9
Killaan	102	111	+8.8
Beefield	21	5	-76.1

This indicates that the wealthier tenants on the better land weathered the Famine well, whereas their poorer neighbours were obliterated. The larger tenants must have benefited from the disappearance of smaller farmers as this meant the vacated land could be incorporated into their own holdings. This included the 2nd Lord Ashtown himself who farmed beef cattle extensively on his own account. These cattle supplied the demand for beef from the rapidly expanding English industrial cities. A new type of farmer began to colonise the Irish countryside: the grazier, a much wealthier, often non-resident, tenant who rented large tracts of land on which to raise beef cattle. While grazing farms existed before the Famine, they multiplied rapidly in its wake as hundreds of small arable farms were swept away and vast swathes of the countryside had more bullocks than people.

This process can be seen at Woodlawn by looking at the population of a single townland between 1838 and 1890. The townland of Tullawicky (182 acres) appears in 1836 in the first Ordnance Survey map showing clusters of houses surrounded by many small fields scattered over the townland. The 1841 census gave a population of seventy-seven with eleven houses, by the 1851 census the population had fallen to thirty-three and the number of houses to five. This trend continued through the late nineteenth century until the 1890 OS map shows the townland divided into a few large fields and only one house. The four inhabitants of this house are listed in the 1901 census as the Cahill family who worked as herders, tending the cattle which were now the only other occupants of the townland. The 2nd Lord Ashtown himself is listed as one of the principal farmers in the townland.

The spread of grazing farms caused much resentment amongst the poor. As early as 1846, the Revd Collis' letter to the Famine Relief Commission contained a bitter condemnation of the 'awful evil' of the present system of land management and asked whether it would be better to break up the pasture land so that farms could be made viable. He also warned of a 'surly growl from the lower classes against what they term the tyranny of the upper classes ... the people here openly declare they will plunder the property of the rich ... the people ... use threatening language'.[113] These warnings were prophetic. In future years the poor would turn against the landlords and graziers in the Land Wars and the pasture lands would be broken up by the Land Acts which followed.

Other changes happened sooner at Woodlawn. Shortly after the Famine, Lord Ashtown got married for the second time, in Yorkshire in 1852. His new wife was the heiress Elizabeth Oliver-Gasgoigne of Castle Oliver and Parlington.[114] Her money allowed him to embark on an ambitious building programme during which the much-admired Georgian house of his grandfather disappeared under a major rebuild in the 1850s, to which the house owes its present appearance (the designs by James Kempster are still in the National Library of Ireland). However, thanks to an exciting discovery by Mr Brian Hull in the archives of the National Media Museum in Bradford, we can now see what Woodlawn used to look like in 1846 on the eve of the Famine. It shows Frederick Trench's copy of the ideal English country house 'in the modern English taste',[115] a pleasant illusion smiling over the tumultuous Irish countryside on which it depended. The next hundred years would see this illusion crumble under the weight of Famine, Land Wars and political independence.

Woodlawn House, 1846. (Photograph taken by Mr Brian Hull from an original calotype by George Fowler Jones. Courtesy of the National Media Museum/ Science and Society Picture Library, Bradford)

5

THE POLITICS OF THE BARONS OF ASHTOWN AND THE WOODLAWN ESTATE, 1850–1923

EIMEAR QUINN, MA

'The Barons of Ashtown and the Woodlawn Estate, 1850–1923' was written under the supervision of Dr John Cunningham, NUIG and used exclusively to produce this paper.

The second half of the nineteenth century was a period of great political change in Ireland. Although the country saw some stability return following the devastation of the Great Famine, tenants began to rise in the 1870s, and this culminated in the outbreak of the Land War in 1879. This mobilisation paved the way for the Home Rule movement towards the end of the century, and the eventual push for independence in the twentieth century. As members of the Protestant ascendency who were loyal to Britain, this mobilisation went against everything the Barons of Ashtown stood for. The history of the Trench family (and later Barons of Ashtown) up to 1850 has been discussed in detail by Bríd Mercer in the previous chapter. The focus here will be on how the Barons of Ashtown contributed to the changing political landscape at both a national and local level, and how this impacted upon the estate in Woodlawn.

The legacy of the Trench family was interwoven with the political history of Ireland long before they received the title of Ashtown. They had fought with the Williamite forces in the Battle of Aughrim and, as discussed in detail by Bríd Mercer, the title of Ashtown has often been linked to the Act of Union and was termed a 'union peerage'. Frederick Mason Trench, who officially became the 2nd Lord Ashtown in 1855, had a political career typical of a landlord of his stature. In the course of his life he served as magistrate, deputy-lieutenant and high-sheriff in County Galway, as detailed in his obituary in *The Irish Times* in 1879.[116] However, he did not seem to be overly active in his three roles at a local level. While the records that survive for the Ballinasloe Poor Law Union from 1850 are quite sparse, his attendance at the meetings of the Board of Guardians was sporadic. Records that survive from June to October 1849 show the Earl of Clancarty chairing the majority of meetings, with Lord Ashtown only attending once in August and three times in September.[117] For 1850, only meetings from February until April are available, where Lord Ashtown attended three out of the seven meetings recorded.[118]

Parliamentary papers do not reflect any more favourably on the 2nd Lord Ashtown. Throughout the nineteenth century, reports were given to the House of Commons relating to the lunatic asylums in Ireland. Lord Ashtown sat on the Board of Governors along with the Earl of Clancarty and Lord Clonbrock. Within these annual reports, a list of the number of meetings attended by governors is given. From 1861 to 1879, Lord Ashtown did not attend one meeting, with Clancarty and Clonbrock appearing at an average of three and one meeting a year respectively. Attendance at these meetings does not reflect negatively on their reputation in the locality, however, as in 1880 Clancarty and Ashtown were noted as providing employment to relieve the distress in the area.[119]

Overall, the post-Famine decades in Ireland were a quite stable time. Relative prosperity, with the exception of a period of depression in the late 1860s, and the lack of a unified tenant movement ensured that politics was rarely at the forefront of a landlord's concerns. Lord Ashtown's second marriage to Elizabeth Gascoigne in 1852 saw his finances greatly improve and the estate of Castle Oliver in Limerick coming under his control. It was this influx of money that saw the large renovation project at Woodlawn get underway. The idyllic Georgian house was transformed, with re-facing in the Italianate style throughout and the addition of two two-storey wings. The new structure, which still stands today, was designed by the architect J.F. Kempster, who was based in Ballinasloe and was accredited with many of the building projects in the town at the time. The railway station house and stores at Woodlawn were also constructed around this time, with the station featuring in the report of the maiden journey on the Dublin–Galway line.[120] Lord Ashtown's main focus seemed to be on building projects, and acquiring and improving his estates. The outbreak of the Land War in the late 1870s saw the first mass political movement since the repeal movement under Daniel O'Connell. By this time Ashtown held over 8,000 acres in Galway and estates in seven other counties, including Offaly, Limerick, Waterford and Dublin. Therefore, before his death in 1879, the 2nd Lord Ashtown had minimal unrest to deal with on his estates.

The outbreak of the Land War coincided with the death of the 2nd Lord Ashtown, and the unrest caused had to be dealt with by his trustees. As his eldest son, Frederick Sydney Trench, had predeceased him, the title moved to his grandson Frederick Oliver Trench who was still a minor. Since Woodlawn had been his resident estate, the absence of an acting landlord should not have mattered much on his other estates in the country. Of these estates, it was the County Waterford one that saw the most unrest among tenants from 1879. This, however, was not necessarily the result of the late Lord Ashtown's rule as he had only purchased the estate in 1875. There were also signs of the Land League involvements on the Limerick estate, with *The Irish Times* reporting how the local branch had forced Ashtown's agent to leave his lodgings.[121] Within the County of Galway there was also general unrest. The estate of the Marquis of Clanricarde in particular saw agrarian violence on a grand scale, including the murder of the landlord's agent near the town of Loughrea in 1882.[122] With the exception of one incident of threatening letters in 1881,[123] there seems to have been minimal agitation among the Woodlawn tenants during the Land War. This general stability was confirmed in 1907 by an ex-RIC man who was stationed near the estate from 1877 to 1885 and stated in the *Irish Independent* that 'there was no outrage committed on Baron Ashtown nor on his property during the Land League agitation'.[124]

After ten years of agent management on all of the 2nd Lord Ashtown's estates, his grandson, the 3rd Lord Ashtown, reached his majority in 1889. Politically, he began his career in the same manner as his predecessor. He took the seat previously held by his grandfather on the Board of Guardians in the Ballinasloe Poor Law Union, and within five years he was named as president.[125] The year 1894 also saw the occasion of his marriage to Violet Grace Cosby at Stradbally in County Laois. Prior to the marriage, the tenants and clergy at Woodlawn celebrated the occasion by presenting Ashtown with gifts including a large silver bowl, silver dessert spoons and two claret jugs.[126] The tenants also reportedly welcomed the couple from honeymoon in March of that year.[127] This form of commemoration was commonplace and does not necessarily reflect stability on the estate, as similar addresses took place in Waterford and yet eviction notices were given to the Clonmel Union regarding nine tenants while Lord Ashtown was still on honeymoon.[128] There are no reports of unrest on the Woodlawn estate and so perhaps the addresses can be taken at face value.

This was not to be the case at the beginning of the following century, as the 3rd Lord Ashtown was to witness great political change nationally, which was to have an influence on all of his estates. The mobilisation that had occurred with the Land League had initiated a nationalist movement on a grand scale, led by Charles Stewart Parnell. Under Gladstone's liberal governments two Land Acts had been passed, in 1870 and 1881, and Gladstone's self-confessed goal was to pacify Ireland. This meant that self-government was a distinct possibility whenever Gladstone was in power. Although Gladstone had passed away in 1893 and the Irish Party had split in controversy over support for Parnell in 1890, the nationalist movement never dissipated and as the century neared its end Home Rule was still on the agenda.

In 1899 the Rural District Council of Ballinasloe was established, and the first elections of the council saw the emergence of a nationalist victory. Lord Ashtown was elected along with three others affiliated with the Unionist cause, but the *Freeman's Journal* attributed this to their individual popularity and not to their political principles.[129] The same paper also printed the resolutions passed at the first meeting of the newly elected Council, now amalgamated with the Board of Guardians.[130] Lord Ashtown chaired the meeting, but lost the vote to remain in the chair to a nationalist by a vote of forty-nine to four. In the duration of the meeting a resolution supporting the Home Rule campaign was also passed. It was only opposed by Lord Ashtown and three others. It was around this time that Lord Ashtown began to focus primarily on politics and the fight against the emerging nationalist movement, including the United Irish League (UIL).

The UIL was established in Mayo in 1898 as an agrarian movement similar to the Land League, and by April 1899 it had not only spread across Connacht, but also emerged as a prominent political organisation.[131] One of the primary objectives of the UIL was to see the breaking up of large grazing tracts and the resulting land divided among smaller landholders. Although Lord Ashtown was renowned for leasing his land to graziers, it was the dismissal of Catholic herdsmen on his Woodlawn estate that caused unrest on a large scale.

With the announcement of the eviction of one of these herdsmen, James Craughwell, in 1902, a large group gathered to voice their opposition. Local branches of the UIL were noted to have taken up the case, as did the local branches of the Herds' Association. The Herds' Association first emerged in Galway in 1882, but saw a revival in interest in 1899 and as its reported activity ceased after 1902, its interests merged completely into the UIL.[132]

Fergus Campbell has carried out a case study on agitation and nationalism in East Galway and found Athenry, Loughrea and Craughwell saw the most disturbances.[133] Woodlawn does not even feature in the discussion, and with the exception of the issues with the Catholic herdsmen, active agitation is not noted on the Woodlawn estate.

Despite the passing of yet another Land Act in 1903, known as the Wyndham Act, Lord Ashtown never sold and actually attempted to expand his estate to the detriment of certain tenants. In 1905 a grazing farm at Clooncah, located to the west of the Woodlawn estate, came onto the market. It was sold by the Estate Commissioners to Lord Ashtown, in spite of the fact that tenants in neighbouring lands had placed an offer. The *Irish Independent* printed an article by T.W. Russell, MP in which he described the case and how Lord Ashtown had intervened and bought the land over the heads of the tenants.[134] The case went to the Court of Appeal before returning to the Land Judges' Court, where eventually Lord Ashtown's offer was denied and the higher offer by the Estate Commissioners was accepted in a ruling delivered in December 1905.

In the same year as the Clooncah case, Lord Ashtown began circulating the journal entitled *Grievances from Ireland* in a bid to garner support in England for the plight of Protestant landed gentry in Ireland. This journal released lists of Catholic clergymen who attended UIL meetings. Outrages such as cattle driving and cattle maiming were documented. Articles against Home Rule and the nationalist cause were published. This ensured Lord Ashtown's political views were now documented on a national scale, but the Woodlawn estate did not seem to rise accordingly. There is little evidence of outrages listed in the Woodlawn area. This is perhaps confirmed further by a speech given in New Inn on 6 June 1907 by the outspoken chairman of the South Galway UIL executive. In his speech, P.J. Kelly, MP, stated that if Lord Ashtown had lived in Loughrea or Kilnadeema, his fate would have been the same as John Blake, the murdered agent of Clanricarde.[135]

Lord Ashtown's unpopularity was growing locally, and his Unionist opinions were circulating nationally, but he was adamant that the Woodlawn tenants were content. In 1907 he gave testimony to the Royal Commission on Congestion in Ireland as a representative of the Irish Landowners' Convention. Within his testimony he stated that he was only attempting to purchase the estate at Clooncah as a counter-measure to intimidation that was occurring at the time. He also stated that there was no intimidation on his own estate, but on those in surrounding areas such as Athenry and Dunsandle.[136]

In the August of that year, a bomb was placed under a window of the Glenaheiry Lodge on the Waterford Estate. Lord Ashtown was staying in the house at the time and the explosion caused significant damage, although no one was injured. The incident occupied the news headlines in national papers, and featured prominently in the House of Commons. Following an inquiry, it was ordered that the District Council of Clonmel pay compensation for the damage, which the councillors questioned on the grounds that Ashtown himself had implicated people from Galway.[137] In an interview after the explosion, Lord Ashtown stated that he had a constant police presence at all times owing to his fight against the agitation occurring in the west, and he believed his opposition in this region was behind the explosion at Glenaheiry.[138] He also claimed that relations between him and his tenants were 'excellent', that they had every opportunity to go to the Land Court, and that they continued to pay their rent 'extremely well'. It was the landlord's belief that his outspoken nature on political issues was to blame for the explosion, and not any tenant unrest.

As 1907 was nearing an end, newspaper headlines once again featured the landlord when the Minnie Walsh case emerged. In this case, Walsh and her 15-year-old son were charged with conspiracy and incitement to murder Lord Ashtown. The case stemmed from anonymous letters detailing a plot to blow up the church at Woodlawn while Lord Ashtown was attending service. Walsh had brought these to the attention of Lord Ashtown's agent and was ultimately indicted in the case herself. The plot never came to fruition, and it was April 1908 before the case finally reached a conclusion. The young boy was acquitted in February 1908, but it was not until that April that Minnie Walsh was finally discharged following a motion of *nolle prosequi* (will not prosecute) by the Attorney General.[139]

The growing agitation did not impede Lord Ashtown's political career. He continued to fund the circulation of *Grievances from Ireland* and in 1908 he edited a book on the Nationalist Party. *The Unknown Power behind the Irish Nationalist Party: Its Present Work and Criminal History* was quite a hysterical piece of writing, its content illustrated by the cover of the cheap edition that featured skulls and a list of words under the caption of 'Past History': 'Blood, Murder, Outrage, Intimidation, Rebellion, Treason'.[140] Within the book it is claimed that the Ancient Order of Hibernians was the 'unknown power' behind the UIL, and the history of the Order is traced back through various Catholic and agrarian institutions including the Whiteboys, the Defenders, the Ribbonmen, and the Molly Maguires (in America). While the publication of the book would have served to raise tensions further between Lord Ashtown and the local UIL branches, it did no damage to his reputation in England as in November 1908 he was elected to the House of Lords 'by sheer unmitigated lottery'.[141] The election had been a tie, and for the first time a clause was invoked by which the name of each candidate was placed in a goblet, with Lord Ashtown's name being drawn and deemed elected. The House of Lords had been the organ of resistance against Home Rule but the second decade of the twentieth century would see their power of veto diminished greatly, and with it the final resistance to Home Rule.

Lord Ashtown continued circulating *Grievances from Ireland* until 1910. In January of that year a parliamentary edition was released, which warned that the alliance of Irish nationalists with the Liberal and Labour parties at the impending election would give a strength to the Home Rule which it had 'probably never possessed before'.[142] It transpired that the election results saw this alliance come into existence as the Irish MPs held the balance of power in the House of Commons. The Liberal Prime Minister Henry Asquith required their votes to pass his social reforms and as a compromise Home Rule was once again back on the agenda. The House of Lords veto had been removed in 1911, so that provided a bill had been passed in the Commons three successive times it would come into law in two years. Home Rule was passed by the Commons again in 1912, but the outbreak of the First World War in 1914 impeded its coming into law. Lord Ashtown's own fortunes were turning along with his political goals, as 1912 also saw him being declared bankrupt. Although bailiffs seized control of his Woodlawn estate, Lord Ashtown managed to get some funds together to ensure a sale did not take place.[143]

At a local level, his political fortunes also faltered with his removal from the Ballinasloe Rural District Council in January 1913. It was noted that he had not been present at a meeting since April of the previous year and as a result the seat should be declared vacant.[144] When it was suggested that Lord Ashtown be contacted for an explanation, Thomas Cahill, elected for the Killaan division along with Lord Ashtown in 1899, insisted against it, stating that no other member would have been tolerated as long. The following year saw the tenants at Woodlawn push for a sale under the Land Act with a report of the tenant meeting stating that Lord Ashtown had not complied when approached by the tenants.[145] In the same year, Lord Ashtown received compensation for the malicious burning of bog in Clooncallis, suggesting that the Woodlawn tenants were beginning to mobilise in a push for the sale of their lands.[146]

While the outbreak of the war in 1914 may have given Ashtown hope that Home Rule could yet be stopped, his personal career took another negative turn with his bankruptcy, which lead to his removal from the House of Lords in 1915. The following year saw his worst fears for Ireland confirmed when the Easter Rising broke out, ensuring that the Home Rule movement would be replaced by a campaign for outright independence. It also was an extremely tough year for him personally, with both his nephew and his eldest son dying on the Western Front. The war effort had clearly not quelled the unrest among the Woodlawn tenants, as in 1918 a meeting of the Ballinasloe Rural District Council commended Jas Cosgrove MP for his attempts to get Lord Ashtown's estate broken up and distributed among the tenantry.[147] Any loyalty to Lord Ashtown that had existed in the nineteenth century had long disappeared by the start of the 1920s. In 1920 Martin Quinn of Clooncallis, from a long-established family on the Woodlawn estate, was elected to the Ballinasloe Rural District Council with the Sinn Féin party.

The political upheaval had yet to subside in Ireland, with 1919–23 seeing an outbreak of extreme violence when the War of Independence was followed almost immediately by a bitter civil war. Big houses on estates were a prime target of the IRA during this time, as they were seen as symbols of the authority the IRA were fighting against. Hundreds of mansion houses were burned as a result.[148] The lodge at Glenaheiry in Waterford was burned beyond repair by the IRA in May of 1920.[149] That July saw the burning of police barracks in County Galway, including the one in Woodlawn.[150] Lewis Perry Curtis utilised third-hand information to date this barracks attack in the spring of the following year. His information also suggests this was a planned attack on the mansion by the IRA, stopped only by the intervention of local republicans.[151] Sources within the locality recite the same story and reveal that it was most likely the aforementioned tenant Martin Quinn who intervened, showing that even in the height of violence in Ireland the Woodlawn tenants still did not resort to extreme measures.

The *Connacht Tribune* advertised a second dispersal sale of many of Lord Ashtown's possessions in January 1922, with over 360 lots for auction.[152] While Lord Ashtown's finances were no longer in a state of bankruptcy, he was still in debt. This sale, however, was not only financially motivated, as the IRA had told the landlord to leave the demesne and the army occupied the house for several months. What precisely prompted Ashtown to eventually return is unclear, but the passing of yet another Land Act in 1923 saw Lord Ashtown forced to sell his Irish estates. At this stage, he was once again resident at Woodlawn and lived there with his family and a greatly reduced demesne until his eventual death in 1946.

Landed estates in Ireland can provide a unique insight into most of the issues that led to the dramatic change in this country in the late nineteenth and early twentieth century. However, on the Woodlawn estate, relations between landlord and tenants were not always reflective of the turbulence seen at national level. As no political movement emerged during tenure of the

2nd Lord Ashtown, he was able to focus most of his attention on improving his estates. A great deal of his expenditure was allocated to drainage, fencing, and the erection of farm buildings, and similar work was actively encouraged and financially supported on his tenants' holdings.

As the 3rd Lord Ashtown took control of his grandfather's estates, he witnessed the powerful status of the landed gentry slowly crumbling. This clearly affected the manner in which he conducted his estates, and his early popularity among the tenants had vanished by the turn of the twentieth century. The 3rd Lord Ashtown showed the same dedication to agricultural improvement as his predecessor, with his expertise even being used at parliamentary level. It was in the world of politics, however, that he was to emerge as a national figure.

Despite his anti-nationalist views causing a stir on the political scene, his tenants at Woodlawn never rose against him. Agitation was widespread in County Galway in the first two decades of the twentieth century, but while incidents occurred on his other estates, the tenants of Woodlawn never mobilised. The emergence of the Irish Free State saw Lord Ashtown's worst fears realised. When he finally sold his various estates he found himself not only without the land that kept his family in power for centuries, but residing in a country where Catholics held the power and the link to Britain was all but severed. However, Lord Ashtown was able to live on his demesne in Woodlawn undisturbed until his death in 1946. Many of the historic buildings erected on the Woodlawn estate are still in existence to the present day and are now places of local heritage, including the mansion, the mausoleum, gate lodges, and the church. This is perhaps a testament to the Woodlawn tenants' temperament throughout the reign of the Barons of Ashtown, even in periods of great unrest on a national scale.

6

THE ARCHITECTURAL HISTORY AND CONTEXT OF WOODLAWN HOUSE

ANNE CAREY

Woodlawn House is the epitome of the romantic abandoned mansion, standing in isolation in its own rambling demesne. What was the main avenue is now a rutted grassed-over track and there is no clear means by which to access the building. The severed social and political context of this impressive building adds to its physical remove. The society it represented was relatively short-lived, beginning with the first flourishing of the country house in the early to mid-eighteenth century Ireland and ending, at the very latest, between the World Wars of the twentieth century or shortly afterwards. Many estates succumbed to penury earlier than this and the establishment of the Encumbered Estates Courts from 1849 arose from the financial difficulties in which many Irish estates found themselves during the mid-nineteenth century. The purchasing of the distressed estates by new landlords continued the social status quo for a few generations more.

In looking at the architectural attributes of Woodlawn House and the architectural context of the building and the estate, the importance of the built heritage of not only Woodlawn but this part of County Galway comes into sharper focus. Just as the landed families existed together in society, so too did their buildings, and any study of a particular house or estate benefits from an appraisal of developments at the time in the wider area. It is in this way that the context is returned to Woodlawn House, as one of the principal estates in East Galway, sitting not in isolation but as a central element in the society of the landed gentry where the ultimate and sometimes ostentatious expression of their position was manifest in their buildings.

The house at Woodlawn is thought to date to the late 1750s, built by Frederick Trench, the grandson of John Trench, Dean of Raphoe, who originally purchased the lands in 1702.[153] Mercer mentions that brief reference was made to a house on the lands in the will of John Trench, in 1724,[154] but nothing more is known about this building and its relationship to the country house inhabited by his grandson from the 1760s onwards. Details relating to the construction of the house at Woodlawn have not been preserved in the historic record, and information of note, such as the architect's plans, or even the name of the architect, cost and exact dates for the building are as yet undiscovered. The physical remains of Woodlawn House are all that survive and it is to those we must turn for evidence.

In national terms, Woodlawn House can be described as a country house of the middle size. Though considerably smaller in scale than the 'great houses' of the early to mid-eighteenth century, this building forms part of the same movement that favoured a return to classical forms in architecture. In Ireland, such 'great houses' as the wide-spreading Palladian splendour of Castletown (1722) by architects Alessandro Galilei and later Sir Edward Lovett Pearce, and beautiful Russborough (1748) by Richard Castle, were seen as setting architectural taste from the 1720s onwards.[155] Palladianism, named after the sixteenth-century Italian architect Andrea Palladio, was an architectural style that drew on the rich architecture of classical antiquity. While political and social factors aligned to allow for a boom in country-house building in the eighteenth century in Ireland, Palladianism, along with neo-classicism, provided the inspiration for these buildings. This phenomenon, which commenced in c. 1716, rapidly reaching perfection in 1722 with the building of Castletown, and continuing until the 1750s,[156] saw architects employed by the principal landowners in the country to enlarge existing buildings on their lands or to construct new buildings to establish an elegant seat for a family rising in wealth and influence. The comparative peace the country saw in the eighteenth century was in stark contrast to the decades of upheaval of the seventeenth century and the fashions that were prevalent in England soon began to show themselves in the landowning-classes in Ireland. Though in total a relatively small number of very large houses were built during this period, numbering approximately twenty-four, the symmetrical and elegant architectural styles of Palladianism and neo-classical architecture were embraced with enthusiasm by the gentry in general, and houses of the middle and smaller size were constructed in their hundreds. Much has been made of the adherence by Irish architects and builders to the classical idiom even in the smaller Irish classic houses, where provincialism was usually absent and the interiors continued the classical theme in a way provincial English houses of the same date did not.[157]

In County Galway, many middle-sized and smaller classical houses were built in the eighteenth century. The lands these houses commanded were often considerable, and large sections of the countryside were given over to demesnes, estates and the smaller holdings of prosperous farmers. The lands of East Galway were divided between landlords of the new Protestant ascendancy and the Gaelic and Anglo-Norman families and they formed numerous estates, which were almost conjoined in some cases. From Ballinasloe in the east to Athenry in the west and from Mountbellew in the north to Loughrea in the south, over twenty-three country houses of middle to small size have been recorded, of which fifteen date to the eighteenth century and among which several are of the size and extent of Woodlawn, including Clonbrock, Monivea, Dunsandle and Garbally. Though the buildings are all individual and unique, they share the characteristic of adherence to architectural styles of the period, largely reflecting the fashion of Palladian or neo-classical architecture of the Georgian period.

Until recently, the elevation of the original entrance front of Woodlawn House could not be determined, due to a lack of pictorial or written evidence. The first-edition OS map (GA86, 1838) provides a very good plan of the building, indicating the central rectangular block of the main house with a recessed single bay to the entrance front and wings with advanced end bays. The layout of the grounds as well as the scale of the farm buildings, which were not extensive at this point, is also recorded. A very valuable and informative photograph of the entrance front to Woodlawn House, dating to 1846, was discovered in recent years and published by Mercer.[158] The photograph was taken from the south-east, beyond the larger of the two water features that were planned on the estate, giving the house, which rises above it among a setting of mature trees, a lofty elegant appearance. This invaluable picture shows a tall three-storey-over-basement country house, comprising double three-sided bows having between them a Venetian window to the first floor and what appears to be a shallow porch or doorcase in stone to the main entrance below. There are end-chimney stacks to the main block and there are single-storey wings, ending in pedimented bays. The façade is dominated by the fenestration, which diminish in size from ground floor to second floor, with a string course between the ground and first floors. The style of the house is Palladian, particularly with reference to the Venetian window, the bows and the wings to either side.

The photograph of Woodlawn records the house just over a decade before the eighteenth-century façade was altered to reflect a different architectural style. In 1860 the 2nd Lord Ashtown transformed the building into a fashionable Victorian villa, externally and internally. The work was designed by J.F. Kempster of Ballinasloe. James Forth Kempster was born in London in 1816 and became County Surveyor for the East Riding of County Galway in 1838. He spent most of the next fifty-three years in this post based in Ballinasloe, where he also undertook private contracts, including numerous works for the Earl of Clancarty both at Garbally and in Ballinalsoe, and a number of works at Woodlawn. In planning the works, which involved remodelling on a large scale, Kempster produced a number of drawings, now held at the National Library of Ireland, Dublin, which beautifully record the rich, sumptuous design.[159] This included the creation of a new entrance front, the construction of a second storey to the wings and the redecoration of the interior. The works to the interior bring the Italianate design boldly displayed on the outer façade to living quarters.

The 2nd Lord Ashtown was not alone in commissioning large-scale alterations to his plain-fronted eighteenth-century house. The fashion from the beginning of the nineteenth century was to give a generous neo-classical makeover to the more restrained of the Georgian houses of the previous century. The first half of the nineteenth century saw more building works undertaken than the second half of the century, due in no small part to the devastating effects of the Famine, though some of the better-off landlords

Front elevation of Woodlawn House. (Courtesy of the National Library of Ireland, AD3590 (2) from drawings and elevations of Woodlawn House, Co. Galway 1859 by J.F. Kempster architect)

used the building projects to give employment.[160] By the second half of the nineteenth century, the Italianate style was the predominant one chosen over the neo-classical form for remodelling earlier country houses.

The use of Italianate style in Britain was first seen in Cronkhill, Shropshire, which was built in 1802 to a design by Regency architect John Nash. This building is a soft, elegant version of a sixteenth-century villa of Renaissance Italy, and as the progenitor of much nineteenth-century house building, it inspired Victorian architects who went on to produce larger, bolder buildings throughout Britain, Ireland, America and Australia. In Ireland the Italianate style could be subtle and understated, as at Tourin, County Waterford or striking and bold as at Glynwood, County Westmeath.

Woodlawn House is a fine example of the Italianate style, clearly bolder than what went before, richly embellished to its entrance front and to the ground floor interior in particular. The decorative elements to the exterior are executed in limestone, with a variety of treatments to the stone to allow for different textures that are used to great effect to provide contrast. The ground-floor entrance front has rusticated stone to the walls of the main block and to the quoins of the advanced end bays to the wings, which contrasts with the vermiculated rustication to the quoins on the first floor. The four fine-carved pinnacles and the corbelled cornices to the parapet, the balustrades to the parapet and the balconettes and the corbelled cornices to the chimneys provide great richness to the building, as do the many styles of carved-limestone surrounds to the windows. The tetrastyle Ionic portico, having four fluted columns, is a wonderful statement, contrasting with the less-ornate Doric columns and Doric pilasters to the tripartite ground-floor windows of both the main block and the wings, the end bays to the wings having Venetian-style windows. The portico also supports a balcony to the first-floor central opening, with cut-stone balusters and a dentilated cornice. The entrance door, which is not original, is round-headed with round-headed sidelights.

Internally, the ground-floor entrance hall and reception rooms as well as the first-floor landing continue inside the confident and bold decoration seen in the entrance front. The entrance hall is broad and high, lit by three round-headed windows in the rear wall. A cantilevered stone staircase, with decorative iron balusters and a ramped timber handrail that terminates in a volute, is a striking feature. Despite the balusters and handrail being incomplete, the workmanship is still impressive. The hallway is symmetrical and comprises two sets of two doorways, all having pedimented doorcases with decorative friezes, flanking a blank niche, on either side of the main entrance door. The hall space is dominated by four impressive Doric columns, two of which are square-plan and engaged on either side of the hallway, framing the stairs behind it. The fine plasterwork throughout the ground floor is still sharp and clear, in particular to the ceilings of the reception rooms that lead from the entrance hall. The ceilings in these rooms are rich in decorative leaf motifs and raised-rib design that still retain their freshness and original colours. The decor elsewhere in the house is simpler and less ornate, though the stairs throughout are always finely finished with stone threads and elegant iron balustrades. The first-floor rooms are very attractively proportioned and decorated, with greater simplicity used for the second-floor rooms. The basement is of course without decoration but it retains much of the atmosphere of functionality, despite poor preservation. There is also a curious attic floor, lit by small windows and comprising tiny rooms with segmental vaulted ceilings.

Kempster's drawings of his work at Woodlawn comprise a front elevation and plans of all floors. The floor plans are annotated, giving the function of each individual room from the basement to the attic rooms. This gives valuable insight into the working of a nineteenth-century country house, with the basement rooms of particular interest. The scale of the domestic operation that was the Irish country house can be seen from the twenty-two rooms in the basement. They included a kitchen, three pantries, a lumber room, a knife room, two cellars, a store room, a turf hoist, a scullery/larder and a dairy. There is also a small storage room denoted as a plate closet.

The hallway of Woodlawn House, looking towards the front.

Another view of the hallway showing the cantilevered stairs.

There were different rooms for the servants, including a men's room, a servant's hall, a sitting room and three bedrooms as well as the butler's room and the housekeeper's room. Beside the housekeepers room was a 'still room'. This room type has its origins in the sixteenth century where it contained a still to produce medicines or perfumes, usually under the direction of the lady of the house.[161] Its use changed over the centuries, as it became more common to employ apothecaries to produce medicines, but this room continued to be linked with an important female personage, usually the housekeeper. In Victorian times, it would most likely have been used to make cake, jams and other preserves and, while appearing as an extension of the kitchen, would still have been under the direct control of the housekeeper.

With the upper two floors devoted to bedrooms, the main social interaction of the house was confined to the ground or 'principal' floor, which had ten rooms ranged on either side of a decorative hall, including one bedroom with an adjoining dressing room and bathroom. There were two small rooms, one serving as a study and the other as a pantry. A further small room was the boudoir, which would have been the inner sanctum for the lady of the house. The reception rooms on the other hand are large and handsome, consisting of a dining room, two drawing rooms, a library and a billiard room. The division of rooms into masculine and feminine areas was part of Victorian life in the country house. The billiard room and the library were the preserve of men while the drawing room was for women, and though they would meet at various times and through various activities throughout the day, they also spent long periods segregated. The floor plans show the strict delineation between the different hierarchies of servants, both male and female, and the different social roles between the men and women in the family.

Country houses were more than just the dwellings of architectural interest; they were communities in themselves. The isolation from urban areas made these houses and the variety of people associated with them largely self-sufficient by necessity. The successful running of a country house relied on a skilful choreography between the family and the large number of servants, living and working within the landscape parks around the houses. The architecture of the wider demesne reveals some gems of composition and design and, according to Rothery, the variety in design of the buildings of the estates in general indicated 'the pleasure which commissioning of these little buildings gave to the architects of Ireland of the eighteenth and nineteenth century'.[162] As a result, Woodlawn House must be seen as just one part of the great estate, albeit a most conspicuous and architecturally grandiose one. The house is surrounded by a wealth of smaller buildings and features, each having architectural merit and reflecting the complex nature of the landed estate. These buildings and features range from the functional farm buildings to the philanthropic schoolhouse to the entirely decorative follies, with a variety of architectural styles and dates that reflect the development of the estate itself.

Ceiling of the reception room, ground floor.

Detail of Acanthus ceiling rose, first-floor landing.

There are representative examples of almost every kind of estate building at Woodlawn, dating from the late eighteenth century to the early twentieth century. Closest to the house are the farm buildings, which lie in an extensive range immediately to the west. The first edition OS 6in map (1838) shows a number of linear farm buildings extending behind Woodlawn House. By the end of the nineteenth century, a more formal range of buildings had been constructed as planned courtyards, extending to the west and south-west. Architect James Henry Webb was engaged by the 3rd Baron Ashtown on various renovations to these buildings in 1907-1908, including rebuilding the stables after a fire and rebuilding the out offices, estate yard and estate overseer's house.[163]

These buildings around the courtyards would have included living accommodation, offices, stables, stock housing and storage sheds. They were not exclusively devoted to the running of the farm but also to the management of household matters. One building of particular interest to the rear of the house was the laundry or linen shed. This building was equipped with deep sinks for washing, high units on rails for the storage and, most innovatively, drying of the clothes was augmented with the building's own heating system. A gardener's house, comprising a two-storey red-brick building to the west of Woodlawn House, was constructed in the early twentieth century, to the west of the courtyards.

Visible from the house to the south-east is a freestanding ice house (RMP GA086:242), dating to the end of the eighteenth century. It is a substantial structure, with a significant above-ground dome and a deep sub-surface element, excavated into a small but prominent hillock. In plan, the ice house is circular and is constructed from a mixture of brick and stone, with fine-cut

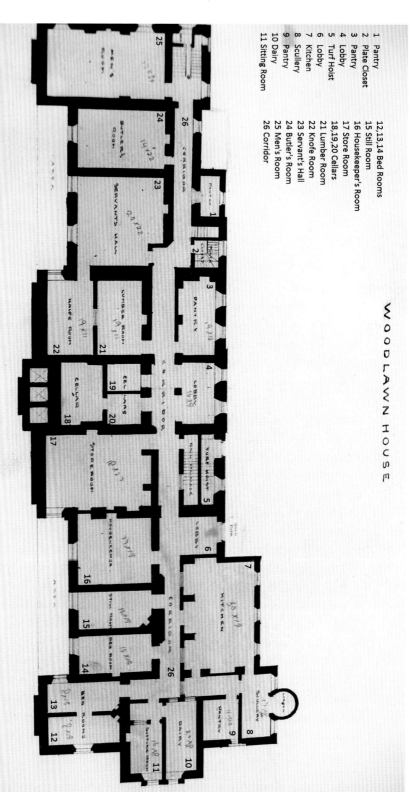

WOODLAWN HOUSE

BASEMENT PLAN

1 Pantry
2 Plate Closet
3 Pantry
4 Lobby
5 Turf Hoist
6 Lobby
7 Kitchen
8 Scullery
9 Pantry
10 Dairy
11 Sitting Room
12,13,14 Bed Rooms
15 Still Room
16 Housekeeper's Room
17 Store Room
18,19,20 Cellars
21 Lumber Room
22 Knofe Room
23 Servant's Hall
24 Butler's Room
25 Men's Room
26 Corridor

Plans of Woodlawn House. (Courtesy of the
National Library of Ireland, AD3590 (3) from
drawings and elevations of Woodlawn House,
Co. Galway 1859 by J.F. Kempster architect)

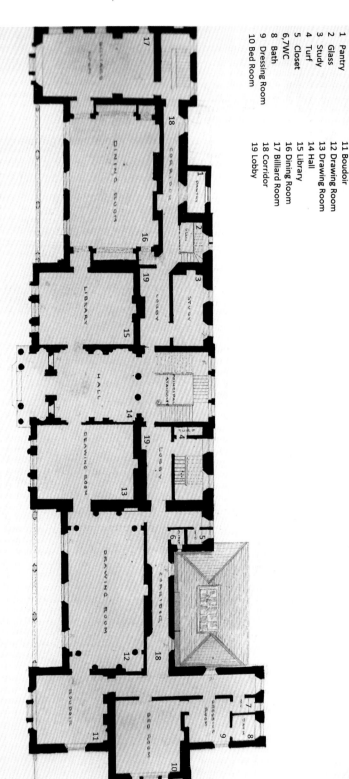

PLAN OF PRINCIPAL FLOOR

WOODLAWN HOUSE

1 Pantry
2 Glass
3 Study
4 Turf
5 Closet
6,7 WC
8 Bath
9 Dressing Room
10 Bed Room

11 Boudoir
12 Drawing Room
13 Drawing Room
14 Hall
15 Library
16 Dining Room
17 Billiard Room
18 Corridor
19 Lobby

stone arches at the base of the dome. Ice houses are known from landed estates throughout the country and many were small, sometimes partly subterranean brick- and/or stone-built buildings used to store ice and to chill food for use in the house. The ice house at Woodlawn is a very impressive example, being larger and more obvious than those on other estates. It is located just under 200m east of the fish pond (RMP GA086:242) and close to the ornamental canal. Close to the ice house is a pair of single-arch bridges, allowing access to what is known as 'Rabbit Burrow Road'. Both bridges have unusual protruding stones to the underside of the arch and neither has a parapet wall, which combines to give them a simple, rusticated appearance. In contrast to this simple style is the White Bridge to the north of Woodlawn House, which is of cast-iron construction and which, along with the main-entrance bridge closer to the house, brings a strong note of elegant design to the demesne.

One of the defining features of the country estate is the entrance and its associated gatehouse, described by Rothery as 'a special building type'.[164] The principal entrance to the Woodlawn demesne is accessed from the road from Killaan Cross to Woodlawn Station. The cut-stone gate piers are recessed from the public road and there is a gate lodge of the classical style (RPS 160),

The ice house (RMP GA086:243) viewed from the south west. It is located at a remove from the house.

which dates to around 1850. A second entrance to the estate is situated to the south-east of the main house, on the road from New Inn to Ballinasloe. In contrast to the classical style of the main entrance, this is a folly-type entrance in the Gothic style, being formed by a pointed-masonry arch set in a rubble stone wall, topped with crenulations and fitted with double-leaf cast-iron gates. To further develop the picturesque medieval-style theme of the entrance are two buildings, also of Gothic style, which flank the pointed archway to the east and to the west. To the east is a plain circular-plan 'sham ruin' tower and to the west is a square-plan, medieval-style tower house, known locally as Grucock's Castle (Recorded Monument GA086: 251, RPS 162). Grucock's Castle was constructed around 1850 as a 'faux' tower house, of significantly smaller size than the building type it emulates. It does, however, contain original medieval stonework, reused to the opes, which are of fifteenth–sixteenth-century date (pers. comm. Christy Cunniffe). It is locally held that this stonework originated in Castlebin Castle (RMP No. GA086:078), in the townland of Castlebin North, which is located approximately 1.6km to the south-west of Grucock's Castle. These lands were in the ownership of Lord Ashtown,[165] but there is now no trace of the castle surviving in the townland. A third gate lodge, situated at what would have been the back entrance to the estate, is now the local post office. This gate lodge would have been convenient for access to the train station.

The crenulated entrance to Woodlawn House with 'sham tower' in the background (RMP GA086:249) in foreground and Grucock's Castle (RMP GA086:251) beyond.

Of similar style to Grucock's Castle is the Gamekeeper's House (RMP GA086: 239; RPS 165), with its conical medieval-style tower set within a bawn wall, located to the north-west of Woodlawn House. Though it has not been surveyed in detail, it appears that this building is largely of nineteenth-century date, though earlier fabric may also be present. There are stylistic similarities to Trenches Monument (RMP GA073:143, RPS 124), the family mausoleum and burial ground, set within an existing bivallate ringfort. The mausoleum is located approximately 1 mile from Woodlawn House. One of the earliest estate features, dating to *c.* 1790, is a folly archway (RPS 120), to the north-east of the house. This 'faux' archway apparently acted as an entrance to Trenches Monument, but without an accompanying roadway it is unlikely it was ever used as such.

Also at a remove from the house are fine stone-built houses located close to the railway station, which were constructed for estate workers. The main station building at Woodlawn Station has been attributed by Sheehy to the country's most prolific railway engineer, George Willoughby Hemans of the Midlands Great Western Railway.[166] The Galway–Athlone line, which was completed in 1851, cut through the northern limits of the Woodlawn estate. To the east of the demesne is the rectory, dating to around 1850 (RPS 159), a detached Tudor-style four-bay structure which was used as a schoolhouse. A number of buildings were added in the 1880s, including farm-workers cottages and a herd house.

The architectural history of Woodlawn House captures much of the history of the built heritage of the Protestant ascendancy in Ireland, from the eighteenth-century Georgian country house to the Victorian remodelling and now to its vacant and vulnerable state. The physical remains and the written sources agree that Woodlawn House was one of the principal houses in East Galway, its owners being part of an emerging group of 'improving landlords' in the latter half of the eighteenth century who used the most up-to-date scientific knowledge to modernise their estates, particularly in the areas of land reclamation, bog drainage and animal husbandry. Other country houses dating to the eighteenth century in the immediate area were also remodelled in the nineteenth century, with the works at Mountbellew in 1820, under the direction of architect Sir Richard Morrison, curiously producing a façade very similar to the Georgian façade of Woodlawn House. Woodlawn has fared better than Mountbellew, surviving into the twenty-first century relatively intact, an enigmatic structure to those glimpsing it briefly from the public road and one which proves to be fascinating on closer inspection. The glimpse inside the house, at the organisation and layout of the building itself, sheds light on the history of the inhabitants and enhances the architecture by giving it meaning and purpose.

Distant view of the (white) bridge on
the grounds of Woodlawn House.
(Dillon family photographs,
October 1835 reproduced courtesy of
National Library of Ireland CLON1993)

7

WOODLAWN CHURCH
AND GRAVEYARD

TOM SEALE

The parish of Woodlawn is made up of five ancient parishes: Kilconnell, Killaan, Fohenagh, Clonkeen, and Ballymacward. Woodlawn Church was designed by Kempster and built in 1874 by Frederick Mason, the 2nd Baron Ashtown. Around 1914 there was a large congregation in Woodlawn. Plans were even being made to extend the church. Alas Woodlawn estate began to decline and the numbers of parishioners dwindled, thus the extension was never needed. (It is interesting to note that between the years 1911 and 1926 the Protestant population decreased in Ireland by nearly a third, compared to a 2 per cent Catholic decline.[167]) During her lifetime in Woodlawn, Lady Violet Ashtown, wife of the 3rd Baron Ashtown, played the organ at the Sunday service and organised the choir. In 1922 the 3rd Baron Ashtown handed the church over to the Representative Church Body.

Photograph taken on the steps of Woodlawn House. Lady Violet is in the centre. (Courtesy of Roderick Ashtown)

Honble ·Frederic Trench   Lady Anne Trench

Frederic Trench and Lady Anne Trench holding a baby, possibly William Cosby, c. 1869.
(Courtesy of Roderick Ashtown)

On inspection of the draft plans one can see a more elaborate church was originally proposed. One proposal was to have a stove within the church with a down-draft which would have drawn the smoke under the floor and up a chimney on an outer wall. This was not adopted at Woodlawn church, but a similar design can be seen in nearby Garbally College, Ballinasloe. A stone spire was also proposed, but a simple slated design was implemented. The building has three stained-glass windows. The east window bears an inscription from the Scriptures. The west window is in memory of the 2nd Baron Ashtown who died in 1880. This window was erected by his wife, Elizabeth. On the south side near the family pew is a stained-glass window in memory of Frederick Trench who died in action during the First World War. He was killed at Beaumont Hamel, France in 1916, and buried in nearby Maillie Wood Cemetery. The temporary wooden cross which originally marked his grave now hangs on the south wall of Woodlawn Church, beside the family pew.

A war memorial on the south wall remembers those from the parish who died serving during the First World War. On the back of the entrance door on the north side is a roll of honour of parishioners who served during the First World War.

Visitors to the church often notice that there are two baptismal fonts. The baptismal font to the rear of the church is the original one. The baptismal font to the front of the church was salvaged from Ballymacward church before it was demolished in the 1950s. The Revd Benjamin Irwin, Rector of Kilconnell from 1886 to 1892 stated that Kilconnell Church contained a font which he described this way: 'The upper part appears to be very old. It is a large limestone block roughly carved outside. It is not unlikely that it may have belonged formerly to the abbey'[168] (before Kilconnell Church was built, the Church of Ireland congregation worshipped in part of the abbey and

Woodlawn Church, 2014.

had to move when the condition of the building worsened). The top of the font is very old and may have come from some older church linked to the abbey and given a new base. On one side can be seen a carving of a scallop shell which is generally the symbol of baptism and an emblem for St James. At Kilconnell Abbey there is an image of St James on a medieval tomb. The friars may have been on pilgrimage there and the scallop shell may have been a way to remember this. Outside the west of the church is a memorial stone to the Hon. F.F.C. Trench who died 1879 and Lady Anne, his wife, who died in 1924. They are buried in the family mausoleum.

Woodlawn church is now part of the Aughrim Union and Creagh (Ballinasloe) Group of Parishes. Services are held on the first and third Sundays of the month.

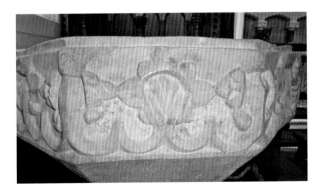

Detail of the baptismal font at Woodlawn church, which came from Ballymacward.

8

WOODLAWN
RAILWAY STATION

MICHAEL JOHN KILGANNON

Woodlawn Railway Station is the centrepiece of the Woodlawn area and has its fair share of history. In 1851 the Midland Great Western Railway (MGWR), was extended via Athlone to Galway, facilitating the opening of the west as a port to America. At a total of 538 miles, this made it the third largest railway line in Ireland. It included the stations of Carrowduff, Ballinasloe, Woodlawn, Athenry, Oranmore and, at the end of the line, Galway.

The building of the railway was done by men with scarcely enough to eat or clothes to wear. These were the years just after the Famine. Their main contribution to the project was their physical skill to hack, shovel and carry huge amounts of broken stone and gravel. The wages were no more than 4d to 6d a day; working hours were long – ten hours a day average, with no diggers, JCBs or loaders, yet they produced a fine structure that still stands the test of time. Many of the men who worked on the railway subsequently emigrated to America and worked on the great railway-building programmes there.

In the 1860s the American travel-writer William Henry Hurlbert wrote:

> Woodlawn Station is one of the neatest and prettiest railway stations I have seen in Ireland – more like a picturesque stone cottage, green and gay with flowers, than like a station... It was hard to believe one's-self within an easy drive of the 'cockpit of Ireland'.[169]

Today Woodlawn is still a characterful station situated at the end of a walled drive overlooked by three pretty period cottages.

Up to the 1970s, all passenger trains stopped at Woodlawn. Then a new order was introduced by CIÉ (Coras Iompair Éireann) which meant that only some of the trains stopped at this station. This policy looked suspiciously like closing the station by stealth and it gave rise to the July 1977 protest against the withdrawal of the 08:30 a.m. service to Dublin. This huge public protest resulted in CIÉ restoring all the train services to Woodlawn and, in more recent years, upgrading and developing the station. Since then a large number of people continue to use the train service from Woodlawn Station. This number is likely to grow in the future, but the current partial service is less than satisfactory and will require continued vigilance by local users over Iarnród Éireann's intentions for the station.

Goods and livestock transport were very important activities at Woodlawn from the earliest times. The old platform across the railway line was organised for loading livestock, which were driven from farms in the Castleblakney or Mountbellew areas, or from buyers and sellers who had animals to trade. In 1860 large numbers of sheep, cattle and pigs were transported via the station. This was reflected in the scene in 1912, when the 3rd Lord Ashtown bade farewell to his prized cattle herd and stud of 200 hackneys on their way to the slaughterhouse in Dublin following their sale to stave off his bankruptcy.

GSWR No.184 leaving Woodlawn
in May 1984. A McDonnell 101
class J 15 0-6-0. It was built in 1879
and is preserved by the Railway
Preservation Society of Ireland (RPSI).
(Reproduced from a postcard courtesy
of Tom Seale)

From the 1930s, huge quantities of sugar beet were transported from Woodlawn to the factory in Tuam, providing an important income for the local farming community.

The dry-goods traffic was centred on the goods store, the biggest building at the station. Goods were loaded and unloaded from the trains and taken onwards by railway lorry to shops in the area, as far north as Kilkerrin. In the store, the stock holding was managed by Christie Fitzgerald, who was also a famous cyclist and is still remembered in Woodlawn. The first cars for sale locally were offloaded at Woodlawn and delivered to local garages such as Paddy Joe Wards. The station closed to goods traffic on 2 June 1978, and the failure of CIÉ to support the goods service is something which still arouses strong feeling locally.

The presence of the station gave rise to the Woodlawn/Railway Hotel, now a private house. A café was also set up on the entrance to the station: it provided light refreshments to travellers in the 1950s and '60s; this was run by Miss May Craig.

A PERSONAL JOURNEY

For us, in our youthful innocence, the world began at Woodlawn Station; it was the place where real life began.

My earliest memory of travelling by train to Dublin goes back to about 1947 when my mother took me to an eye specialist, Professor Lavery, in Fitzwilliam Square. The school medical service had picked up that my sight was uneven, and that I had a squint in my left eye. My mother wasn't taking any chances, so she and I set out for Dublin from Woodlawn Station. Train carriages in those days were divided into a series of compartments each holding about ten people, seated five facing five. There was a corridor along the length of the carriage. All this was wonderful to me, but the journey seemed very long. Our destination was Westland Row Station; up to the 1930s, or thereabouts, all western trains had their terminus there. We stayed overnight in Dublin and returned home the next day. For my first railway experience from Woodlawn, crossing the Shannon in Athlone was a highlight of the journey. How lucky I was to have such a wonderful amenity almost right on my doorstep!

In 1949, my Uncle, John Kilgannon, came home from the US for the first time in forty-five years. It was a happy but poignant visit, as a lot of family history was revisited. He came to Woodlawn Station with the inevitable trunk full of goodies on 10 May and left on 29 June. He was so special – a warm, loving man through whom goodness shone. Woodlawn Station was his point of departure and I was broken-hearted.

But years passed, and in August 1959, I was on my way to Dublin; this time for a Civil Service interview. A man whom I had known from previous years was in front of me at the ticket office. 'Where are you going?' came the enquiry from inside. Quick as a flash came the reply, 'Straight through to Euston'. How many hundreds of others stood in the same place and got their tickets for Euston or Queenstown en-route to the US, Canada, Australia or New Zealand? How many young men went to fight in foreign wars? And how many of those never returned?

Railway stations big and small dotted the country at one time from Donegal to Kerry and made the most remote places accessible. But passenger traffic was only a part of their stock-in-trade. The transporting of goods of all kinds was maybe an even bigger dimension of the railway system, and our station more than held its own with the best of them. It wasn't for nothing that Woodlawn's huge goods store commanded the station entrance.

Railways, including our own, have featured many times in spectacular episodes including 'The Great Train Robbery', the rescue of Sean Hogan at Knocklong Station in 1920. Woodlawn witnessed the tragic shunting accident in the 1930s when a man was killed there, and also the quick thinking of

Special Steam Train passing through Woodlawn, 13 May 2002.

Martin Hillary who got over the railway gates to take a seriously ill child to Dr Murphy nearby.

There is the famous case of Thomas Cahill, a man wrongly accused of serial murder in the US, who was extradited to America via Woodlawn Station. American police arrested him at his home in Tullawicky and took him to Woodlawn Station in 1873 for a number of murders he did not have hand, act or part in, to return and stand trial in Dorchester NY. But for the confession of the true culprit, Piper, Cahill would have been hanged as, through an unfortunate series of coincidences, he was the prime suspect. A narrow escape indeed. Truth is often stranger than fiction. The documentation of this case, which I heard of first from Cahill's grand-niece Bridie Hillary, was supplied to me by Sean Griffin of Keave, himself a relative of Thomas Cahill. When eventually discharged, Cahill returned to Ireland and arrived at the house to find it completely empty. Not even a chair to sit on. He went outside, took a stone from the wall,brought it in and sat on it. Life hardly gets much tougher than that. He lived on, got married and died in 1910. He is buried in Killaan Cemetery.

Irish Railways began in the 1830s with the first line running from Dublin city to Dún Laoghaire. Comparatively speaking, railways are a recent arrival on the transport scene. In Ireland, many companies got in on the act quite quickly. The big ones, GNR (Great Northern Railways), Great Southern Railways and Midland Great Western, provided the main trunk services within the country, while dozens of satellite companies served the outlying towns and countryside. County Galway got its first rail service in 1851 when Midland Great Western extended the line from Athlone to Galway. The railway was not for most ordinary people at the time. Money was too scarce to be spent on such luxuries. The main customers were described as politicians, clergymen, cattle jobbers, landlords and their minions.

The goods store was a hive of activity with wagons being shunted in and out and huge boxes piled up waiting to be delivered by the railway lorry as far away as Kilkerrin on the north side or to Loughrea in the south. Martin Dooley drove that lorry until ill health overtook him; he died a young man. Jim Moran followed Martin Dooley as driver, and Jack Mullen later still.

Today the station is basically the same as when it was first constructed. Recent developments include the provision of a loop, which is a siding to allow trains to bypass each other, and an upgraded platform, as well as toilets and a heated waiting room. It is a well-appointed transport facility. The major issue of the moment is to provide a southern platform to facilitate passengers travelling eastwards. There is a good service to Galway, which is used constantly. The fine nineteenth-century stone structures of the station are still intact. It has long been thought locally that the railway came to Woodlawn through the influence of the 2nd Lord Ashtown (Frederick Mason Trench), the local landlord. There is no evidence to support this theory. Firstly, Ashtown was not on the Board of Midland Great Western, the deciding body for railway operations. The nearest member was Daly of Dunsandle. From a geographical point of view, Woodlawn lay directly on the route between Athlone and Galway, so it was a natural location to provide a service. Ashtown did give 12 acres of land to facilitate the railway, but it suited him to have the railway running almost within sight of his house. It should be borne in mind that Woodlawn then, as now, served a huge hinterland and initially was the nearest service point for Loughrea, as the Loughrea branch from Attymon did not exist until 1896. The Midland Great Western Company operated the line through Woodlawn until they were taken over by CIÉ, which later became Iarnród Éireann.

The railway's own architect George Willoughby Hemans designed Woodlawn Station. He was working from a clean sheet, as before 1851 Woodlawn was open country. Construction work on the railway line and station commenced about 1848/49. The station was built at a cost of £3,279. The building of the railway was on a contract basis of 5-mile sections with labourers' payment for work done at 10d to 1s. It was back-breaking work with exposure to the elements. The work involved cutting through embankments, hauling sleepers, building bridges and culverts, fencing and laying down the permanent way. The end result, as we can see today, is testimony to the skill and dedication of all who worked on the project. Their work has stood the test of time.

An ancestor of mine, John Callanan of Loughclarebeg, Gurtyryan worked on the railway construction. The railway-building era was one of high-quality stonework. At the same time as the railway, a new church was being built at Ballymacward under the patronage of Dr John Derry, Bishop of Clonfert. A few years later, around 1860, Woodlawn House, home of Lord Ashtown, underwent massive reconstruction with two large wings added. These projects involved huge amounts of stonework and it is quite likely that a number of the same craftsmen worked at all three locations.

The Irish Railway network was fully operational for about sixty years. Huge sums of money were invested by the wealthy who were the equivalent of today's bondholders, but in later years many of the smaller lines proved uneconomic and were closed. Among these was the beautiful scenic line from Galway to Clifden: Padraig Pearse used to travel on this line on his way to his summer-holiday home in Rosmuc. Another railway casualty was the famous

West Clare Railway, immortalised by Percy French in the song 'Are You Right There Michael?'. CIÉ embarked on a widespread closure policy in the 1970s exemplified by the closure of the entire line from Athenry to Sligo. Stations too were axed: for instance, on the main Dublin to Galway line the stations of Carrowduff and Oranmore went. It was a short-sighted policy and deprived the country of vital pieces of infrastructure.

Woodlawn stayed unaffected by these cutbacks until the 1970s, when CIÉ introduced a policy of restricting services and in July 1977 the morning service was withdrawn without notice. A public protest was organised, which resulted in the train being stopped and brought widespread media attention. It has taken a huge investment of time and energy over the years to ensure that Woodlawn retains its passenger service, and the campaign is still ongoing.

The station did wonders for the population enrichment of the area. As there was no local experience of train management, in the early years of the railway staff came from elsewhere in the country. Many came and went; others came and stayed. A series of stationmasters occupied the station house and from there controlled the entire operation. Their names are still remembered today: names such as Jimmy Mullen (who himself worked at the station); Rutledge

Woodlawn 1974, County Galway by O'Dea, James P. (1910–1992).
(Courtesy of the National Library of Ireland ODEA 119/2)

and Mallon, to name just a few. The stationmaster was boss and his word was law. When a train arrived, he appeared on the platform in full livery, and he was the visible sign of authority. His uniform and cap set him apart as a person to be reckoned with. He was responsible for all activity at the station including the keeping of records, money receipts and payments, answering queries and maintaining good order at the station. Stationmasters were moved, depending on their performance, to more important posts such as Athlone or Galway on promotion. They were the company representatives on the ground. Woodlawn stationmasters were generally well liked and respected by their staff.

The station master had a number of important staff members under his control: signalmen, porters, and goods-store staff. Many of these became permanent members of the Woodlawn community; they brought new ideas and fresh thinking with them, as new arrivals always do. The Daly family of Monaveen originated from Michael Daly who came as a signalman from Mullingar about 1910. He married a local Quinn girl and lived the early years of his marriage in what later became known as Katie Kelly's, now Frances and Tony Cummins' home, in Whitepark. Later, he moved to Monaveen where he spent the rest of his life.

Tom Martyn worked as a signalman at Woodlawn. A signalman had a highly responsible job, as on him depended the safe movement of trains through the station. Working from the signal cabin, he had control of the signals situated at the approaches to the station east and west. Farthest out was the distant signal, which had two positions: down to indicate 'off' and up to indicate 'on'. When the signal was up, the oncoming train had to stop; down meant it could proceed. This signal was at least a half-mile distant from the signal cabin and was operated by a cable stretching the full distance. You would need to be strong to operate this signal from such a distance. Tom Martyn was a thorough gentleman. He lived in one of the signalmen's houses adjoining the railway. Tom retired about twenty years ago and went back to live in his native Loughrea. I believe his mother lived with him in Woodlawn for some time before he retired.

An old established landmark at Woodlawn Station was the café run by May Craig. The origins of the café are not clear to me; it was a pre-fab type of structure constructed of galvanised iron on a concrete foundation. May was a member of the Church of Ireland community and a lovely old lady. She provided a valuable service by selling tea and cake to weary travellers from places like Mountbellew, Moylough and more distant parts. The place was always warm and welcoming. But May's service did not stop there. The café was also a news agency supplying the daily papers, which in the

Peter Mahon and Tom Martyn in the signal cabin at Woodlawn, Sunday 28 August 1983.
(Courtesy of Des Doherty)

case of my family came in a bundle of four to Raftery's shop in Monaveen, later to become the Monaveen Inn.

May also carried a considerable stock of magazines, books, comics – the Beano and the Dandy were all the rage. Magazines dealing with women's problems were kept under the counter and were not for general distribution. One magazine which May Craig stocked was *The Irish Home*, published by Kill Avenue, Dún Laoghaire. I had the ecstatic experience of seeing my name in print for the very first time in *The Irish Home*. There was a children's corner which had some competitions and I entered and won! The prize was a half crown, which was as good as winning the Lotto today. The café is long since gone. May had lived a solitary life in the middle one of the three beautiful houses that face the station. Her father had been an RIC constable, but where he came from or who his wife was I do not know. The police station was nearby on the opposite side of the road into Carrowmore. May grew old and frail and she died in St Brigid's Hospital, Ballinasloe. I believe I shed a tear for her as a lovely human being who I am sure the Lord has taken to himself.

There were Jim Kett and the Kett family. Jim was a Limerick man who came to Woodlawn as a signalman having had a couple of earlier postings on the railway. His name was confusing for us as we thought it was Kitt, as in the Galway version. But Jim set me right on that ... The former Kett house now stands vacant; the family have all moved on. The Mullen family had a substantial presence at Woodlawn Station for many years. Best known was

Michael, known as Mick, who filled the position of stationmaster in the years when the service at the station was being curtailed. There was Jack who worked on the railway lorry delivering goods to a wide hinterland and who later drove the lorry himself; and there was Jimmy, part of whose railway career was at Woodlawn as a signalman/gatekeeper.

From the beginning of the rail service, Loughrea was part of Woodlawn's catchment area, a situation which continued until the opening of the Attymon branch line in 1896. From then on, Loughrea passengers and business had their own service and the Woodlawn link dried up. The Attymon line continued to operate until the early 1970s when it was closed but, although Loughrea no longer had a rail service, the Woodlawn link was not re-established to any extent.

There is, however, significant usage of the station by places south of Woodlawn. North of the station there is considerable daily passenger traffic which is consistent and growing. This area has been the strongest support and demand for the Woodlawn rail service. Taken as a whole, the station catchment area extends for approximately 15 miles both north and south, and for 5 miles east and west, giving a service area of 150 square miles. For all of this area, Woodlawn Station is the only public-transport system available, hence the necessity for its maximum usage. The campaign to promote and develop Woodlawn Station is based on this potential.

The development of the station by Iarnrod Éireann in recent years has been favourably commented on by locals. The extension and renewal of the northern platform, the upgrading of the waiting facilities, the car-park development, have all greatly enhanced the appearance of the station. These developments,

Looking north-east showing the stores, signal cabin and signalman's house at Woodlawn, 2015.

however, are but half the Woodlawn story. At present, Woodlawn serves the Galway traffic mainly, and there is a good morning, afternoon and evening service which is used by up to thirty people per day. The absence of a service eastward, especially a morning train that would get passengers into Dublin by 10 a.m., is a major handicap. The extent to which it would be used can only be established by putting the service there. It did exist for 125 years. The one factor which would eliminate the technical issues is the reconstruction of the southern platform allowing trains eastward- and westward-bound to take passengers. Currently a Dublin-bound train stops at 10 a.m., which is welcome.

In any event, the campaign to secure a full rail service at Woodlawn will continue. Strategically located as it is between Athenry and Ballinasloe, it is as important today as it was in 1851.

IN CONVERSATION WITH MICHAEL DALY

My granddad worked on the railway all his life. Maybe ... 1875, he was born. He started in Mullingar I suppose in about 1890 or – at a fairly early age anyhow. Probably about 20 years in Mullingar before he came to Woodlawn and he worked for 30 years in Woodlawn as a signal man. They worked long hours. I think they used to even work the seven days of the week. Whatever way the rota worked, you had got to go to work every day. Early duty, maybe mid-day duty, evening duty, you were always working. The Midland Great Western Railway, I know that. I think I remember him talking about 48 shillings a week. Would that have been the wages?

I'd say he was always in the signals that type of thing. It was a responsible job. He was probably cycling ... to that signal box at all hours of the morning, starting maybe at three o'clock or half past three in the morning. How he came to Woodlawn – would he have got a vacancy or something, I wonder? I think they transferred him. Because the late Jim Kett, anyhow, who succeeded my grandfather – he always listed about six or seven places he worked in before he finally came to Woodlawn. He came there in 1934. He always mentioned Ennis, Foynes, Carlow, Charleville, so he was in a lot of places around the country before he finally came to Woodlawn. I think he was a kind of halt keeper – that's what they used to call them in those days. They had something to do with passengers and getting your baggage ready to go on the train. There would be more baggage on the trains in those times. And my father took over from my grandfather then as signalman because my grandfather retired.

Paddy Quinn, my uncle-in-law, used to be a ganger on the turf. They used to draw it by horses to the station and put it on wagons or open trucks, for Dublin, I suppose. And of course I remember the goods trains coming there. I remember the store and Mick Mullin working in it. Anyhow, when I'd be coming home from school, Jack, Mick's brother and Paddy Kenny, were on the railway lorry. They'd be bringing stuff down to Mountbellew. I can't say that I remember Christy Fitzgerald. I can't really remember him now but I remember Mr Carroll was the stationmaster, anyhow, and his sons were working there at the store; I think they were clerks. I remember Jack Ward and PJ drawing stuff from the station with a pick-up truck. They'd be loading stuff up there off the bank when I'd be coming from school back in the 60s. There'd be stuff going down to Ted Raftery's shop that would have come. The Railway lorry would have brought stuff down there as well.

IN CONVERSATION WITH JUSTIN MITCHELL

The railway cottages:

They were never Railway cottages. They were Estate cottages, belonging to Lord Ashtown. They were built for employees of Lord Ashtown's Estate and the people that lived in them were tenants. And in most of the houses except one, there were two families living in them. There was two stairs in the two end houses. The middle house was owned by the Creggs.[170] Cregg himself worked in a kind of senior position up in the House and, Lord Ashtown, when the station came to Woodlawn, built a small café just outside the station and he rented it to Creggs' daughter, May, who was slightly deaf. She never married and lived down in the house across the field. She used to come up every day and open the café. She had an agency from Eason's in Dublin and she sold the morning and evening papers there and all the different magazines. May gave teas and coffees to people who might have to wait one or two hours for the train to arrive. The trains could be up to two hours late because they were steam trains. They could be held up for any reason. Bad war years, when you would pull into Ballinasloe, there might be so many wagons to be taken off or put on or something else. And tomorrow, he might be on time so you had to be there. May Cregg served the tea and coffees there, maybe sandwiches as well. She had one table, so she could seat four. It was only very small. And she sold cigarettes.

The cottages were facing south. You'd be exposing the back of them, the yard, to the station otherwise. Those houses are beautiful stone, a gem to look at.

The people living in them all worked up in the Estate. The extended O'Brien family who are down in Monaveen, Gorteen and Killaan are branched out in different places and some of them got on very well in life, married and had families. They all came from that house, the last descendent of the O'Brien's.

IN CONVERSATION WITH BRIGIE KELLY, THE GATEKEEPER

I was lucky a vacancy came up in Irish Rail just across from the post office. That was as a gatekeeper. I worked eleven years there. You had to be on time first going off, and then you had to attend to the gates. They were great big gates at that time. Tilly lamps had to be looked after. They had to be done every week. Lamps had to be taken down. You'd have to go up to the post office for a ladder to go up to the signal to take down the lamp and clean it. They were wick lamps. The lamps on top of the railway gates, had to be done once a week as well. You had to keep a watch on gate glass for if you got a strong wind, the wind could blow out the lights and that could cause an accident. The odd tractor wouldn't see anything if there'd be no lights for them to see, so you'd have to be very alert for the lights on the gates.

And the station then had to be kept neat and tidy and lawns cut and flowers sown. I worked there long hours, one week from quarter past five in the morning until half four in the evening and then there would be another shift from half four in the evening till half one, half two in the morning. There was only two of us employed at that time. Then they rotated the hours better and they took on an extra person, so we had just roughly six hours.

We had two distance levers, two and half, almost two miles out in each direction, the Ballinasloe side and the Athenry side. We used to have to walk up out there with our lamps, full of paraffin and ... that had to be done once a week. And then the home lights, they were just beside the cabin there. It was all staff. When I left there it was all changed over so I was the only member on staff that did it. So 'twas a very busy time. I'd say when they got the staff, it was in full swing. There was Jimmy Mullen and Ida Seale in the signal cabin at that time. Then there was talks of going automatic so that meant the gate keepers weren't needed. The signal was going to be worked automatically from Dublin. And it did come. So the barriers are there today and they're minded by Dublin automatically. They need nobody.

A CONVERSATION WITH JOE KEANE, WHO WORKED IN WOODLAWN FROM OCTOBER 1983 TO APRIL 1988

I was a signalman for about two years until Mick Mullins retired. I applied for his job and was successful. Now, getting that job meant that I was no longer on shift work and I didn't have to work any nights. My job then was roughly from half seven in the morning until three o'clock in the day, office hours. The only thing was that it was seven days a week. Again, it was the only job in Ireland I think at the time, with CIÉ, that when you got promotion, you actually got a reduction in your pay. I lost my shift allowance, which was an extra day's pay in the week. I got promoted, but my wages went down. It's laughable but this is the ways things worked then. The only advantage was that I was at home every night. Okay, I had to work every Sunday but that brought my wage back up again because I got double time for Sunday work.

But anyways, as I say, when I transferred to Woodlawn, I was a bit dubious about whether or not I was doing the right thing, the place being so quiet. There was not many trains servicing the station then. On Monday mornings there was the 6.30 a.m. *Early Bird* leaving Galway stopping at Woodlawn at 7.05 a.m. The 8.13 a.m. from Galway did not stop in Woodlawn. The first train from Heuston Station in Dublin to Galway stopped in Woodlawn around 10.10 a.m. The next train to stop in Woodlawn was at 12.10 p.m., the train from Galway to Heuston. So as you can see, there were a lot of quiet moments.

Having said that, there was plenty of callers to the cabin – you know, people would come in for the aul' chat. A retired signalman there at the time, Jim Kett, he really kept an eye on us. Poor aul' Jim reckoned he was still in the job and he sort of thought he was over us, and he'd be coming up and checking our Train Record Book to see what time the trains went during the night and all this sort of thing. Then every now and again, we'd play a trick on him. We'd turn over the pages and he might be looking at maybe a month behind and he'd say 'How the bleddy hell's that? That couldn't be right!' you know. We used to play all sorts of tricks on him just to confuse him but he used to take it in good sport.

9

WOODLAWN POST OFFICE

DES DOHERTY

Based on information from
'Aspects of Galway Postal History 1638–1984', by Jimmy O'Connor.

In the late sixteenth century the post was carried by the cavalry. This system was very unreliable for the general public.

By 1635 Thomas Witherings was appointed postmaster of England. In 1638 he sent Evan Vaughan as deputy postmaster to Ireland to encourage a post service. He appointed post stages along the main roads from Dublin. By 1653 posts were established to Belfast, Coleraine, Derry, Sligo, Galway and Cork.

In 1659 the route through Maynooth, Mullingar, Athlone, Ballinasloe, Loughrea, Galway, with a branch route from Athlone, Roscommon, Boyle and Sligo was known as the Connaught Road. Other routes were the Cork Road and Ulster Road. Letters were carried by post boys who walked miles a day or went on horseback. By 1764 post was received at Galway from Dublin on Monday and Thursday and dispatched on Tuesday and Friday.

In 1657 Oliver Cromwell introduced the first Post Office Act. It established one General Post Office for the three countries and fixed more reasonable charges.

By 1711 Queen Ann posted a new bill. It reset postal charges and established a system of inspections to check on deliveries, post boys and so on. This new act also changed the postmaster system. Up to this point, the owners of ale houses and inns were the highest bidders for the business of collection of mail. When the post boy stopped at their establishment, a crowd would gather, which was good for business.

Mail coaches were introduced to Ireland in 1789. A service between Dublin and Galway commenced in 1809. This service was provided by private owners.

The coaches were often robbed and two armed guards were required on each coach for protection. By 1813 a third guard was provided during the winter months on the Cork, Limerick and Galway coaches. The Galway coach left the Royal Mail coach office at Dawson Street at 8 p.m. every night. The route was through Kilcock, Clonard, Kinnegad, Mullingar, Athlone, Ballinasloe and Loughrea. By 1847 the dawn mail left the GPO Dublin at 8 p.m. and arrived in Galway at 10.46 a.m. taking fourteen hours and forty-six minutes. The UP mail was dispatched from Galway at 2.14 p.m. arriving at Dublin at 5 a.m. This coach passed through Oranmore, Craughwell, Loughrea, Aughrim, Ballinasloe, Athlone, Moate, Kilbeggan, Tyrellspass, Rockford Bridge, Kinnegad, Clonard, Enfield, Kilcock, Maynooth, Leixlip and Lucan.

While towns on these routes received a mail service, the villages and towns in between did not. In 1815, Charles Bianconi started a cross service between towns. His first was from Clonmel to Cahir. By 1842 he serviced eighty-two towns in Ireland. Some of the Royal Mail coaches he operated in Galway were Ballinasloe to Roscrea via Banagher; Ballinasloe to Castlebar via Tuam; Clifden to Galway; Galway to Limerick via Ennis; Portumna to Roscrea via Cloughjordan.

By 1850 he started a four-horse coach service between Mullingar and Galway carrying ten passengers. With the completion of the Dublin/Galway rail line in 1851 the mail was now carried by train at a cost of £500 per annum. There were two dispatches and arrivals between Dublin and Galway. Up to 1680 there was no postal systems in London. That year a private penny post was established. One penny for deliveries in the city and an extra one penny for deliveries to outskirts.

By 1832 William IV legalised the establishment of penny post office in Ireland. In a short period of time, 295 post offices were established with 27 in County Galway. A letter/parcel had to be less than 4 ounces and only official Post Office letter carriers were allowed to carry mail. This system had its faults as well as the receiver also had to pay for the letter. Those less well-off did not want to see the post boy at the door. Rowland Hill, secretary to the Post Office, reformed this system by introducing a minimum rate of one penny for a letter weighing up to half an ounce. Postage was paid by the sender by means of an adhesive stamp to prove that postage had been paid. The stamp had a profile of Queen Victoria and was printed in black for letters weighing up to half an ounce. The twopenny blue was also introduced for mails up to 1 ounce. Rowland Hill also introduced the slit in the door to save the post boy time. In 1901 the postmen were given cycles to deliver the post. There was an allowance of one shilling a week for cleaning and repairing of the cycles. Deliveries on Christmas day ceased in 1936 and deliveries on Saturday ceased in 1978.

To relieve pressure of the sorting office in Dublin, the Travelling Post Office (TPO) was established in 1887. A carriage was designed as a sorting centre. A post office was established at Woodlawn on 6 April 1853 just after the opening of the railway line. At this time, the post office was on the railway grounds. From 1887, mail was delivered to all local areas from Woodlawn by horse and cart. There were also three dispatches from Woodlawn – two by TPO and one to Ballinasloe. The earliest Postmaster at Woodlawn that's on record was Susan Robinson 1901. By 1911 she had married Robert Sheirson. The post office was then moved to where it is today. The story goes that Lord Ashtown had to pay for his telegrams as he was outside the one-mile area for free delivery. So he had the post office moved across the road to his back lodge. It is believed that around this time the Sheirsons bought the back lodge from Lord Ashtown. Ethel Sheirson then took over from her parents. When she got married to local farmer (Daw) Kelly from Carrahulla, she put the back lodge up for sale and P&T put the post office up for tender. The post office assistant at that time was Eileen McLoughlin from Ballynabanaba, Kilconnell. She had qualified as a postal clerk in Drogheda. She met and married Kevin Doherty from Carramore, Woodlawn on 6 February 1951. They sold their house at Carramore and bought Woodlawn Post Office in 1954. They applied for the post office tender and were successful in their application. Eileen was postmistress until her death in 1977. From 1977 to 1983 Marcella Mitchell was acting postmistress. Chris Doherty took over at this time and is the current postmistress. The sorting office at Woodlawn Post Office closed on 29 July 2013.

Paddy Hession and Celcus Sheridan outside Woodlawn Post Office, 29 July 2013. This was the last day that the post was sorted at Woodlawn for local delivery.

Brendan Sheridan with his mother Ellen (née Hogan) on his first day of service as post-man in the early 1940s. (Photograph taken at Clooncagh; reproduced with kind permission from his son, Celcus, the current postman at Woodlawn)

The following are the postmistresses and the years they served:

Year	Name
1901	Susan Robinson
1911	Susan Sheirson
1911	Ethel Sheirson
1954	Eileen Doherty
1977	Marcella Mitchell (acting)
1983	Chris Doherty

The following is a list of post office assistants, full-time postmen and temporary postmen:

POST OFFICE ASSISTANTS

Ellen Robinson, Mary Tansey, Robert Sheirson, Noreen McLoughlin, Breege Carr, Una Flannery, Brigie O'Brien, Mary Egan, Terry Hanlon.

FULL-TIME POSTMEN

Francis Turner, Kelly Loughrea (part of the local group that built Woodlawn Dance Hall), Bill Monaghan, Bill Burke, Bill Lesley, Brendan Sheridan, D.J. Coffey, Celsus Sheridan, Seamus Dilleen, Johnny Furey, Pat Gavin, Paddy Hession, Paddy Kelly, Mattie Brien, Lisa Doherty, Bart Doherty, Danny Attwood, John Ryan, Michael Coen (post boy).

TEMPORARY POSTMEN

Michael A. Kelly, Michael Bellew, Martin Collins, Marie Melia.

The above list is from memory only. My apologies to any person I have omitted.

According to Woodlawn NS Roll book 1914–1922 a Mary, Henry, James and John Broderick's parent is registered as postman, residence Monaveen.

Dates of post offices opening in the local area:

Ahascragh	1810		Kilrickle	1852
Athenry	1786		Kiltormer	1840
Attymon	1891		Lawrencetown	1834
Aughrim	1813		Loughrea	1638
Ballymacward	1861		Menlough	1851
Bullaun	1883		Mountbellew	1848
Caltra	1861		Moylough	1832
Cappataggle	1881		Newbridge	1899
Castleblakeney	1733		New Inn	1857
Colemonstown	1899		Portumna	1797
Gurteen	1876		Tuam	1726
Kilconnell	1805		Woodlawn	1853
Killoran	1949			

BRIGIE KELLY

Brigie Kelly (*née* Brien) worked in the post Office at Woodlawn from 1962 to 1971. She was raised in one of the three stone houses near the station.

I went three years to the Technical School in New Inn. I cycled up every morning and home every evening. After that, it was the Group Cert that time. Then I enquired for a job. I went to my local post office and I asked the postmistress there and she took me on for a month, on trial. I ended up – is it eight, or nine, years there? It was a busy, busy time and I enjoyed every day of the post office. Every week I worked in it was lovely. 'Twas long hours but we were delighted to have a job. There was no big wages that time. It wasn't there to be paid out.

The counter was very busy that time. There was no public kiosk. 'Twas inside the post office and anyone that wanted calls made would have to come in and book the call through the assistant at the counter and they'd have to get through to head office in Ballinasloe. The telephone exchange was there, and we had a switchboard and we used to have the switches turned down at eight o'clock, I think. Eight to ten at night, plus Sunday. I think it was nine to eleven on a Sunday and seven to nine Sunday evening. Yeah, that had to be done. But that was it. There was a shop in the post office. There was never an idle moment. Everything was written down and everything balanced out at the end of the week or the end of the evening for the shop.

Oh yes, there was a separate money box for our own shop. 'Twas nearly always cash. Shopping was nearly always of a Children's Allowance day, or of a Friday; Pensions. They would buy their groceries then. 'Twas busy. Keeping the shelves stocked up, and the usual.

I used to start at quarter to eight in the morning and work until maybe half ten at night. They were long hours, yeah. You couldn't go home till the switchboard was finished. All the switches had to be turned down and then the shop was open there bringing money in. 'Twould be often half ten or eleven o'clock before you finish. I used to do the housework too. The kids were young and the postmistress wasn't in the best of health.

The post office hours were from nine to six that time, yeah. And there was a half day of a Thursday. Still, the switch board had to be looked after till ten o'clock. There was national calls and local calls made and all of them had to be noted and kept written into a book at the end of the month. It was all sent into head office, Ballinasloe at the time. Irish Rail was Telephone Number 4; Number 5 was Doctor Murphy; Number 2 was Mitchells, Justin and Tommy Mitchell; Number 6 was Mrs Raftery of the pub, Monaveen; Number 7 was Mr Trench; Number 8 was Ted Raftery and 9 and 10 was Coillte. We had what – four trunk lines to Ballinasloe? It took four lines to get through to Ballinasloe: one, two, three, four. We had two lines to New Inn and a line to Gurteen and we had a line to Kilconnell. New Inn was very, very, busy – there was always nice demand for Garvey's.

The switchboard opened at 8 o'clock in the morning. There was one particular time there was a neighbour – Thomas Mitchell. He was in a Dublin hospital and he was pretty ill and of a Saturday evening his son rang me to know would I mind ring in the morning a little earlier. They had their own phone in their house but that was no good for they still had to get through to the exchange and the exchange was in Woodlawn in the post office. The switchboard shouldn't be in until eight o'clock but due to the emergency, I had to ask the postmistress herself and she said yes. So I came up in the morning and I put up the switches. I opened it roughly at quarter past six and, as I say, it shouldn't be opened till eight. I rang Mitchell's and I said to one of the boys there, 'Give me the number and I'll just work from there.' So I got the number and got it through and they got the sad news that the father had passed away. It's so different now. You can just take the phone out of your pocket and get through direct to all those places.

We had no problem with Derek Trench's accent. We would always see his number 7 dropping down when he'd ring. The cover would drop down and we would come through the kitchen very fast – we mightn't come as fast if it was the Doctor that was ringing. Oh yes, Derek Trench used to come down with his horse a couple of times a week and come there to the gate, the entrance gate now to Des Doherty's house and turn around there and back up again. Might come in for the paper. He was a lovely man. And she was a lovely woman, Mrs Trench. She'd come down many's the time.

We used to have telegrams that time and we used to have to get our bicycles and head off – 'twas, I think, it was five miles, or seven miles, as the rates that time. We would often have to go up to Woodlawn House with the telegrams, bring the bag into the kitchen. Use the back entrance, yeah. You daren't go to the front. I don't know – was it five or seven? – I think it was seven miles that time you wouldn't have to deliver a telegram. For under a mile it was cheap. Yeah, 'twas for pittance that time, a few pennies. Many's the time we wouldn't get it.

The bicycles were supplied by An Post. They were collected at the post office at the time. They had to have a shed there especially for them. The postmen were Bill Lesley from Tooreen, Woodlawn and Bill Monaghan from Cappataggle. They would cycle down every morning doing their rounds on their bicycles. Bill Lesley had from Killaan – I'm nearly sure he started in Killaan and he had go down below into Keave. He used to go into Divilly's in Keave and he used to hate to see letters for it because it was way down the fields. Oh, they had a big area. He'd be gone out, say, roughly nine in the morning and wouldn't be back till half two or three o'clock. So they had a fair run. They had a mail bag then to go on the twenty past four train that time from Galway to Dublin, then to the GPO. And our postman used to be back – he'd always be back and bring it up to the train for us. If he wasn't back then you'd have to do it.

Oh yes, back then Woodlawn was busy. And that was nothing until Christmas time would come. A fortnight before the Christmas, or maybe a week before the Christmas, you'd be handling forty or fifty turkeys and geese and ducks and heads out and legs out, all going to England. Oh yes, it was very busy. The mail times used to be in the evening at 6 o'clock and the post office then would close right after that. They were long days and Christmas was very busy as well because you had to have an awful lot of heavy bags both incoming and outgoing. 'Twas tough work.

After nine years I left the post office, two months before we got married. We got married in '71. Married a local man. Lived in a place called Moyarwood, Woodlawn, a few miles away from the station. We started a family and we ended up with three kids.

10

EDUCATION IN WOODLAWN

MARIAN DEELY AND TOM SEALE

HISTORY OF EDUCATION IN WOODLAWN

MARIAN DEELY

Irish people have always taken pride in education, and giving the gift of learning to a child is an honour that many take for granted today. At times education took a back seat when there was 'real work' to be done at home, either on the farm, gathering potatoes or saving turf. But education was always important, and most parents would do without before depriving a son or daughter the chance at the books.

The evidence for schooling in Woodlawn goes back to 1770, when Frederick Trench applied to the Royal Dublin Society for a grant to construct a school in Woodlawn.[171] The first-edition Ordnance Survey map (1839) (Galway, sheet 86) shows a 'National School' marked immediately south of Killaan Graveyard, on the border of Cloverpark/Cloonamorris. The area known locally as 'The Village' is visible to the south with an abundance of houses. Larkin's map (1817) of Galway (see page 54) also shows a building at this location, which we could presume is the national school shown on the later map. This corresponds with school records at the National Archives which state a school was established 'around 1820', at Woodlawn.[172]

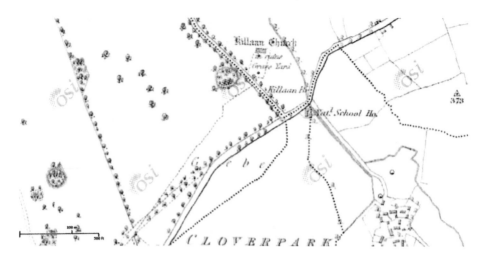

Extract from the first-edition Ordnance Survey map of Galway (Sheet 86) showing the location of a National School House in Cloverpark, south of Killaan Graveyard and Church.

Records from 1833 state the school was made of stone and had a slate roof. The dimensions of the school were originally 26 feet by 12 feet but later had an extension added of 20 feet by 11 feet by Lord Ashtown. The only source of annual income for the school came from Lord Ashtown in the amount of about £30. Attendance in the school was more male-orientated, the average believed to be seventy pupils in total all year through. An application for aid from the state and a request that Woodlawn School be included in the National System is signed by Protestants and Catholics. Not all names were legible and apologies for any mistakes in deciphering the writing:

Protestants	Roman Catholics
Wilm Trench	Mark Hughes R C. Rector
John Trench	------- Donellan
---- ----------	------- Nolans
J. Harrison MD	William Devane
J. Anderson	Michael Gradin
John McCulla	James Fahy
Joseph Hall	Dudley Cannon
T. McCulla	Pat Raftery
A. Harvey	Batt Duffy

In a letter dated 10 September 1833, from Michael Donohue, Woodlawn, to William Trench, Education Board, Merrion Street, Dublin the application for the inclusion of Woodlawn School in the National System is discussed. The population of Killane parish amounted to '1,317 souls'. It was decided that the present school had limited capacity and was too small. It was also the intention of Revd Hughes to make a second application for the erection of a school in Grange parish.

Records show that the Education Board at the time was quite diligent in their inspections of schools. An inspection on 25 May 1835 shows 114 males and 94 female scholars with a further inspection on 4 November 1836 stating that 'the school was conducted with much order, efficiency and discipline'. Henry Waide was a teacher in the school at this time.

Boys and girls were taught separately. Both schools were in the same building. The boys' school was under the board from 19 September 1833. The following were the rules set out on 14 April 1846 for Woodlawn Female School:

> This school is to be opened in summer at half past nine o'clock a.m. and to remain open until half past three in winter. The hours are to be from 10 until 3 o'clock. Saturday is to be set apart for religious instruction, the forenoon for the Roman Catholics, and afternoon for the Protestants. This instruction is to be given only by the Minister for the respective religions provided they think proper to attend for that purpose. On the other five days of the week the scripture and tracts of the Education Board are to be read during school hours by those children who are sufficiently advanced but the ministries are strictly forbidden to enlarge upon any points of religion which are not held in common by all sects of Christians. Catechism and other books including any particular form of religion are not to be listed in the school on any day excepting Saturday. The education in the other respect will be the usual elementary ones with instructions in needlework and the Books ... especially those recommended by the Commissioner of Education. No book is to be used in the school without the direction of Lord Ashtown or his Agent. The school is open to the public on all days of the week for the purpose of inspecting the register books if using the method of instruction and ascertaining that the rules are faithfully observed, but the business of the school is not to be interfered with by visitors.[173]

The following is an application to the Commissioners of Education for aid towards payment of teachers' salary and the supply of books dated 10 November 1847.

The school is in the same building with the Woodlawn Male School which is already under the board. The Female school was then taught in the hours when the teacher resided. New Woodlawn School has since been finished and the Female School taught there since October last 1847. The house is about three inches from Kilconnel on the western side.[174] It is new, built of stone, bricked inside, and slated. The Female school room is 7 × 25 feet. The furniture is new, metal stands and Mary Foreman, aged 24, trained in 1844 as teacher. The average attendance in October is 59. Saturday is set apart for religious instruction. The school is under the management of Lord Ashtown and the layman of the Protestant Church of Ireland.

Signed

J. Trench

November 10th 1847

The new school that is mentioned here is possibly what is now known as 'The Rectory'.

In 1852 the school closed due to the need for a teacher. Eliza Nylie was hired on a salary of £15. She had been a pupil teacher in Coleraine DMS (model school). In 1855 there were twenty-six children present at the time of an inspection. The average number of children on the rolls for the last twelve months being sixty-two, average daily attendance for last twelve months being 30, average age was 9 years old with thirteen children under 9 years of age and eight children 11 years and over.[175]

In January 1877 there was an application made for a classroom assistant which was rejected on the grounds that there were insufficient numbers for such an addition to the staff. At this time there were two people working in the school – Robert L. Foreman as a teacher and Elizabeth (Eliza) Foreman as a work mistress. The application was made on behalf of Roberta J. (Josephine) Foreman, age 17, to be appointed assistant teacher. The internal dimensions of the classrooms at this time were 32ft by 18ft and 25ft by 18ft. If appointed, the plan was to have Miss Roberta Foreman teaching in the classroom 32ft by 18ft. The attendance records for the school were as follows:

	Male	Female	Total
No. of children now on rolls	37	50	87
Average daily attendance for last quarter	25.3	33	58
Average daily attendance for preceding quarter	25	33.3	58
No. of children present on day of visit	20	22	42

However, it was determined that an assistant should be in the school instead of a work mistress as the attendance did not entitle the school to both.

A new school opened on 2 August 1886. The school was built of stone walls and had a slate roof. There were two classrooms. The internal length, breath and height of each room were 26¼ft by 15ft by 11ft. Both rooms had floorboards and a fireplace for heat. The school grounds were enclosed by a wall. Mr P. Corry was appointed teacher for the male school. He was schooled in Cooraclare National School, County Clare and taught English in the bishop's seminary, Loughrea. Margaret M. Byrne was appointed teacher for the female school. She trained at Baggott Street and came with high recommendations from the reverend mother.

Woodlawn Male National School, Roll number 12910, was inspected on 11 October 1886. It was noted that the school was open Monday to Friday from 10 a.m. to 2.30 p.m. in summer and that the teacher was Mr Patrick Corry.

Class	Students Present
Infants	17 boys
1st Class	5 boys
2nd Class	5 boys
3rd Class	2 boys
4th Class	2 boys
5th Class 1st stage	1 boy
5th Class 2nd stage	1 boy
Total boys present at time of inspection	33 boys

The teachers listed in record ED2/37/275 were as follows:

Teacher	Dates
P. Corry	2/8/1886–15/4/1888
Patrick Duggan	14/5/1888
Patrick J. Frost	1893–1895
John Lillis	1896

Grants for Woodlawn Male National School were suspended from 30 September 1899, the average attendance having fallen below twenty, and there being sufficient accommodation for the male pupils in the female school. The boys continued to be taught separately in their own schoolroom in the hope that the attendance would increase, until 18 September 1900, when the two schools were amalgamated and taught under the teacher of the female school, Mrs Anna Cahill.[176]

The Church of Ireland school, which was in what is now known as 'the rectory', was still in progress at the turn of the century. According to the school roll book, Ashtown Male and Female National School, Roll number 15,719, Circuit 12, Section B, in the townland of Killaan, was built on a site of thirty perches in 1846/1847. It is not clear if this is what is now known as 'the Rectory'. Its Patron was the Rt Hon. Lord Ashtown, Woodlawn, County Galway. The correspondent was the Very Revd Provost Crawford DD, The Rectory, Kilconnell, County Galway.

In the Daily Report Book, visitors were invited to enter their names, the dates of their visits, the number of pupils present and 'such opinions as they think fit on the state of the school'. The numbers did not exceed twenty in any given day of inspection, and were as low as eleven on one occasion. The following is a record from the Daily Report Book 1904:

> I have been present at the teaching and spelling classes and find that the lessons have been well prepared – October 13th; There are 18 pupils present – girls at needlework – the sewing is very neat. V. Ashtown, M.S. Crawford, October 13th.

School roll books show transfers from Ashtown School to Woodlawn Male and Female Schools up to the year 1922.[177] Long-serving teachers at Woodlawn include Miss Henchy, Mrs Mulvehill, Mrs Cahill, Miss O'Neill, Ms Duhan and Mrs Lally. After almost 200 years of education in the locality, the last principal to close the doors in Woodlawn National School was Ms Edel Dwyer in 2014.

TOM SEALE

I started school in the old national school building in 1953. I was about five years old. The teachers at that time were Mrs Mulvihill in the senior room and Miss O'Neill in the junior room. The Mulvihill family lived beside the school in the teacher's residence. Miss O'Neill lived in Ballymacward and drove to school in a Ford Anglia car. Living near the school, my brothers and sisters and I were able to go home at lunch and while I was in infants I would get home at two o'clock.

The playground in the old school was very small and was divided in two halves. The girls took the left half and the boys the right half. In the wintertime it would be very muddy from all the running about and if someone fell they got covered in mud. There was no running water at that time and you had to wait to get home to clean up. In the summertime it was dry and the ground was hard but there was never much grass to be seen at any time.

Each room in the school had a separate hallway with rows of hooks for hanging coats. At the back there was a bin for storing fuel. The school was heated by open fires and each parent was expected to supply either a cartload of turf or a bag of coal. When a parent came with turf the boys would be sent out to carry it in the bins.

Every few years a doctor and nurse would come and we would get a medical examination. A dentist would come and examine our teeth and extract any decayed ones. The dentist's chair was made out of steel and could be folded up for transportation. When someone got a tooth out they were sent home and at that time everyone walked to and from school. It was not very nice walking home with a sore mouth. After a few of these dentists visits one learnt to volunteer to be one of the first patients and get home instead of waiting in dread all day to be called.

Every few years there would be outbreaks of mumps, measles and chicken pox. One by one pupils would complain of being sick and show the usual symptoms. The teacher would then let them go home. Sometimes so many were missing with an epidemic the school would be closed for a few days.

There were rumours of the building of a new school but they were not taken too seriously by us because they had been around for some time. But then one day site clearance began. The contractors were a local firm – Thomas Mitchell & Sons. We watched with interest every day on our way to school as the new building took shape. In contrast to the old school, the new school had two large bright classrooms with enough desks for everyone to sit down. No longer did classes have to stand when other classes needed the use of the desks for writing. There were toilets with running water and separate cloakrooms for coats. Outside there were a play shed for wet days, a large playground and also a surfaced play area. It was a big change from the old building. Even though the new school was complete, we still remained in the old one until one day to our great delight Mrs Mullvihill announced that we would move to the new school. We took our schoolbags and walked down the road behind our teachers and into the new building. That was in 1958.

Sometimes showmen would come to the school and do a show. It would be announced well in advance and we would have to get sixpence or a shilling from our parents to cover. They would do some magical tricks, sketches or maybe a Punch and Judy show.

In sixth class, the primary certificate examinations took place. They would be supervised by a teacher from outside the school and were regarded as a serious exam at that time. Some people stayed on and did it in seventh class, but most finished their primary-school days after the primary certificate exam.[178]

Woodlawn National School, 1948. From left to right, back row: Miss McManus, NT, Mona Kelly, Gertie O'Neill, Sheila Burns, Nonie Moran, Theresa Naughton, Josie O'Neill, Sara Murray, Mary Burns, Mary Kelly, Miss O'Neill, NT. Second Row: Ann Malon, Margaret Burns, Cathleen Carney, Rita Brien, Annie Brien, Judy Bellew, Maureen Brien, Essie Quinn, Ann Kitt, Mary Carney, Cathleen Dolan, Ann Murphy, Mary Moran. Third Row: Pauline Dunphy, Carrie and John Raftery, Tommy and Paddy Moran, Joe Dolan, Frank Murray, Justin Mitchell and Eric Kett. Fourth Row: Sean Quinn, Colm Malon, Mickie Dunphy, Michael Brien, Joe Malon, Jackie Mitchell, Tony Bellew, Sean Murphy, Gerard Mitchell, Gabriel Murphy, Bobby and Michael Mitchell.

Woodlawn NS Senior Class Students 1960. From left to right, back row: Mary Burke, Maureen Biggins, Emily Madden, Mary Daly, Vincent Sheridan, Ambrose Mitchell and Mattie Brien. Second row: Mary Kelly, Carmel Biggins, Mary McDonagh, Mary Glynn, Paddy Quinn, Angela Quinn, Denis Madden, Gearoid Mullvihill, Tom Seale, Raymond Barry, Anne Murray and Michael Daly. Third row: Helen Pritchard, John Joe Brien, Joseph Sheridan and Tony Kett. Front row: Helen Sheridan, Watt Pritchard, Michael Bellew, Josaphine Brien, Paddy Kelly and Michael McDonagh

Woodlawn, New Inn and Bullaun Confirmation Classes, 1969.

Woodlawn, New Inn and Bullaun Confirmation classes, 1974.

Woodlawn NS Sixth Class, 1987. From left to right, back row: Cathal Barry, Lorcan Byrne, Michael McDonagh, Josephine Lally (Principal), Ivan Kenny, Richard Seale, Paul Seale. Front Row: Emer Barry, Elaine Kenny, Lisa Doherty, Eibhlin Quinn, Melissa Kelly.

Woodlawn NS Students 2002/2003. Teachers: Josephine Lally (Principal), Mary Murray and Maureen Duhan. From left to right, back row: Louise Glynn, Danny Biggins, Michael Glynn, Drew Doherty, Grainne Kenny. Middle row: Amanda Glynn, Cliona Biggins, Caoibhe Kenny, Christopher Sheridan, Gary Hennelly, ? Barrett, Gerard Dwyer. Front row: ? Barrett, Aoibhinn Kenny, Orla Doherty, Margaret Sheridan, Brian Duhan, Ailbhe Duhan.

Woodlawn National School Students 2013/2014.

11

NINETEENTH-CENTURY EMIGRANT LETTERS

MARY GORMAN

For many centuries Irish people have left our island to seek a better life on foreign shores. Almost every family in our country was affected by emigration. Up to the early 1920s, this hardship was the outcome of oppressive colonial rule, where the landlord's dictate left tenants barely subsisting or evicted and out onto the side of the road.

Up to the late 1960s, it was a common sight to see an emigrating son or daughter on the platform of Woodlawn Station surrounded by family. They would wait together for the Galway to Dublin mail train that pulled into the station at 4.20 p.m.

As that train pulled out of the station there would be the most mournful weeping as the family watched it disappear into the distance with their loved one who, up to the 1930s, would, most likely, never be seen again. A broken-hearted son or daughter would strain their head out the window of the moving train looking back to their beloved family on the platform until the family disappeared in the distance. Turning back into the carriage of the train, all the emigrant was left with was memories of home; damp mornings, bright summer days, saving the turf and hay, the perfume of the heather lingering. These are the memories that would sustain them during their lifetime on foreign shores.

The train went right into Dublin and from there another train took them to Dún Laoghaire where they boarded the boat to England. These were the lucky ones because they may be able to make the journey home for visits. Over 200,000 are estimated to have gone to England to help in the war effort. Half a million people emigrated from Ireland in the years between 1946 and 1961.

The majority of these were UK-bound. Permission was required to leave the country, as recalled by Michael Carney:

> I remember I had to go to Loughrea to get a permit to travel. The superintendent had to sign it. I had to tell him I was going on holiday. At that time the authorities did not want farm workers leaving the land. It was after the war and they wanted the crops saved. At the end of January 1949 I arrived in Manchester.[179]

Those emigrating to America, Canada or Australia, even up to the 1930s, rarely returned. 1,872,000 Irish-born are listed in the American census in the year 1890. This is more than half of the population in Ireland at the time. On the night before their leaving, an American wake was held to bid them farewell. Emigration was akin to death. Bereft, they made their way to Cobh in Cork where they boarded the ships bound for New York, Montreal, and Sydney.

But emigration had its advantages. Despite the heartbreak of leaving, emigrants settled in new countries where they found work through their links with the large Irish communities that had been established in England, America, Canada and Australia. These Irish communities were crucial in supporting their members who often faced anti-Irish feelings. The Irish were known to stick together, through employment, marriage, and contributing to their new communities through sports and music. Their descendants would later forge pathways into the professions and politics.

Many emigrants sent money home to help those they left behind and this money became integral to the Irish economy. Families at home could pay the rent to the landlord, avoiding eviction. They could purchase necessary items for the running of the land and household. Younger siblings could be educated. Anne Marie Byrne recalls her own personal memories:

> I can still see my Mother wiping away her tears during the rosary as we knelt in prayer to keep her girls safe in foreign parts. Her own sister had gone thirty odd years before. Indeed, she lived to be 103 years and never again set foot in Ireland. America was far away then, having to travel by ship, but it had the draw of the 'Land of Opportunity and of the Free'.
>
> It still tears at my heart when I think of my beautiful sister, ten years my senior, leaving home to join our older sisters in England. Of course, England wasn't too far away, but then two years later she returned to attend her American Wake. I recall the bus load of people, family, neighbours and friends going to Rinanna (now Shannon) Airport. The bus was full of fun,

laughter, song and even music as our friend, Paddy, played the accordion all the way there. A good send off to support them on their journey to the unknown. But the return journey was a far cry from glee. The tears flowed and consolations were meted out but it was only the beginning of the desolate feelings that followed in the weeks and months thereafter.

The parcels and dollars in the post helped to soften the blow a little, but the inner despair was still that as I wondered what had I done to cause her to leave? The excitement was palpable for weeks when we knew she would be coming home. All the stops were pulled out, every corner was cleaned, and paint brushes were in view as the place was got ready for the yanks. She was like a film star in our eyes with makeup and the best of clothes and money flowing. Her generosity knew no bounds, treating all of us, and turning us out in great style. Yes, the rewards were great on the outside but then the day came for the return trip. It was time to relive the pain all over as we bade goodbye for long years again.

We are very fortunate to have letters written to and by local man John Kelly from Carahulla, Woodlawn, who immigrated to Australia in the 1800s. These letters are a fascinating account of the meanings that can be assigned to emigration, from longing to hear news from home, establishing friends, to the heroic efforts made by emigrants to prosper.

The farm holding now occupied by Mary Dempsey (*née* Kelly) can be traced back through the family to 1856 where John Kelly (carpenter) is listed as 'Head of the House' on Griffith's Valuations. His son William Kelly (1825–1892) was the next to run the farm, followed by his son William (1864–1935) and followed by his son Michael (1906–1990). Michael's daughter Mary and her husband now live on the farm.

The earliest evidence of emigration from the household arises in the mid-1800s.

Letter X, written by John Kelly, Constabulary, Coolrain, Queen's County (Laois) to his brother Joseph in Carrahulla, dated 24 January 1854, documents an intention by Joseph to emigrate to Australia. John relates that an inspector who visited his office recommended such a move, as he had a brother and uncle in Australia who were doing well. John and Joseph are sons of John Kelly listed on Griffith's Valuation and the brother of William (1825–1892) who continued to farm in Carahulla. Joseph Kelly followed through with his intention to emigrate and was followed by his brothers, John and Richard.

Letter from John Kelly, Constabulary, Coolrain, Queen's County to his brother Joseph Kelly, Carahulla, Woodlawn 24 January 1854.

Coolrain, January 24/54

Dear Joseph,

I once more take up my pen to let you know of my safe arrival on the same day that I parted you. Hoping that you and cousin William had arrived in the same state. Dear Joseph, indeed I had being home in very good time. I had very great luck. The day had been very wet just as I did arrive it did rain very constant the remainder of the day. I had the Officer out on his inspection on yesterday and indeed he had made a very strict inquire for my Father and Mother and Brother and hoped that they were all well. I told him that they were all well and that you had a great notion to emigrate to Ostrelia. He says you could not do better. He has a brother and an Uncle in that country and that they do give a very good account of it and they would encourage any man to emigrate that possibly could go. You will give my best respects to all the family and my most gracious thanks for all their kindness to me during my visit. No more at present but remains your truly Brother until Death.

John Kelly Constabulary
Coolrain

Mr. Joseph Kelly
Carrahulla

Letter Y from John Kelly to his parents in 1861.

Rutherglen Post Office
New South Wales,
Australia.
23rd August 1861

Dear Beloved Parents

It is with great pleasure I hasten to answer year long looked for letter which I received on 18th instant and nothing on earth gives me greater pleasure that to hear that ye are all well. I am writing this letter to ye from a locality which I never wrote before. I am residing now for the last three months, 40 miles from Beechworth and within one mile of Joseph and Richard and half a mile from William. He has share in a claim on my Property which I gave him and he is in hopes of making a big pile out of it. They have a

steam engine at work and it took a great deal of capital to purchase the
land for claim and in ... I sold the land in shares, 16 shares for £160 and if
it does turn out well, I will lease about ten claims more. So please God, I will
be able to make about £1000 out of it and will not injure the land. I have
stuck to the force as yet, as Mrs Kelly is not getting her health at all. She is
living at bushworth with her brother. Herself and Margaret Raftery. I will
expect a letter from them over this evening and I am making preparation
to see to him. They removed to Beetheyh. Please God I will have the whole
lot of them down in the course of a month. Richard, Joseph and William
is well. I do go see them very often Mrs. Kelly was on a visit with Joseph
for a week. Herself and Mary Ann which is getting to be a fine girl and the
other Lizzie remaining in Beechworth. She is getting to be a fine girl also.
Mrs Kelly's sister did not arrive as yet. Mrs. Kelly is getting very uneasy on
account of not hearing from her which I believe is the cause of her bad
health. She frets so much on her account but I hope ere long that she will
arrive. I have not got a letter from her brother this six months whatever
must be the cause. I do not know it might be waiting until he will supply
more with the requisite. Information on his sisters departures from home.
I hope all the family is well and in good health. I was very sorry to hear of
Patrick Raftery junior being so unwell on account of his tooth ache. I have
never got a tooth ache as yet, thank God. Margaret Raftery's uncle, Michael
Kelly was on a visit here with Joseph about a month ago. He is well and a
very steady man. You always make great delay in not answering my letter.
I was very much disappointed when I received a letter for Margaret the
last mail. I slipped my thumb under the sail to have a good read and to my
surprise there was not the least ... from ye but the address on the envelope.
I was very angry (_) and (_) the one turn and she had a letter one month
before me when you would be addressing a letter to me again you ought to
mail it only to my care. I hope my mother is well and in good health. Also
William and wife and their two youngsters. I hope the day will come when
his and mine will be old playmates. William says he will not write home
until he will send a golden letter. I am at Joseph and Richard to write home.
Their farm is making a good deal of money for them. They do be up with
me every mail to know all the news. No more at present until I hear from
you again and still remain
Your (_) and affectionate son

John Kelly
(WJ Kelly)[180]

NOTES

1 Ryan, M., *Irish Archaeology Illustrated* (2001), p.31

2 Bennett, I., *Excavations Bulletin*, www.excavations.ie

3 Gibbons, M., *The Irish Times*, 26 April 2014

4 Waddell, J., *The Prehistoric Archaeology of Ireland* (2000)

5 Ryan, M., 'An Early Mesolithic site in the Irish Midlands', *Antiquity*, vol.54 (1980), pp.46-47, in http://heritagecouncil.ie/unpublished_exavations/section3.html

6 Collins, T. and Coyne, F., http://irisharchaeology.ie/2013/03/a-mesolithic-cemetery-irelands-oldest-burials/#sthash.wTLDW2wW.dpuf) (2003 & 2006)

7 See more at: http://irisharchaeology.ie/2013/03/a-mesolithic-cemetery-irelands-oldest-burials/#sthash.wTLDW2wW.dpuf

8 see chapter 2

9 Powell, P., 'Megalithic Monuments of Ireland', *County Guide Series Volume XVI Galway* (2012), p.47

10 www.excavations.ie

11 O'Toole, L & O'Flaherty R., 'Bronze Age Halberds and Cranes', *Archaeology Ireland*, Spring 2011, Issue 95, p.13

12 Mitchell, G.F., 'Studies in Irish Quaternary Deposits: No 7', *Proceeding of Royal Irish Acadamy. Section B: Biological, Geological and Chemical Science*, vol.53 (1950/1951) pp.111-206, www.jstor.org

13 Raftery, B., *Pagan Celtic Ireland – The Enigma of the Irish Iron Age* (2000), pp.64-81

14 Waddell, J., *Kockagur, Turoe and Local Enquiry*, pp.130–3

15 Kelly, Eamon P., https://www.academia.edu/3206867/Bodies_from_the_Bog_New_Insights_into_Life_and_Death_in_Pagan_Celtic_Ireland (2015)

16 www.archaeology.ie; O'Floinn (1995), p.227 (pers. comm. M. Cahill and M. Sikora, NMI)

17 All known archaeological monuments are issued with a Record of Monument and Places number

18 All archaeological testing and excavations are issued with a licence number

19 McKeon, J. & O'Sullivan, J. (eds), *The Quiet Landscape* (Dublin: NRA, 2014), p.111

20 Mallory, J.P., Moore, D.G. and Canning, L.J., 'Excavations at Haughey's Fort 1991 and 1995', *Emania*, vol.14 (1996), pp.5-20

21 Doody, M.G., 'Ballyveelish, Co. Tipperary', in R.M. Cleary, M.F. Hurley and E.A. Twohig (eds), *Archaeological Excavations on the Cork-Dublin Gas Pipeline 1981-1982* (University College Cork 1987), pp.8-35

22 Doody, M.G., 'Ballyveelish, County Tipperary', in R.M. Cleary, M.F. Hurley and E.A. Twohig (eds), *Archaeological Excavations on the Cork-Dublin Gas Pipeline (1981-1982)* (Wordwell; Bray, 1987), pp.8-35

23 J. Waddell, *The Prehistoric Archaeology of Ireland, Second Edition* (2000), pp.206, 216, 269

24 Grogan, E., *The North Munster Project*, vol.2 (Wordwell; Bray, 2005), p.111

25 Raftery, B., 'Irish Hillforts', in C. Thomas (ed.), *The Irish Sea Provence* (1972), pp.37–58; CBA Research Report 9 (Council for British Archaeology, London)

26 Raftery, B., *Pagan Celtic Ireland: The Enigma of the Irish Iron Age* (Thames and Hudson; London, 1994), p.38

27 O'Sullivan, J., 'The Quiet Landscape: Archaeological Discoveries on a Road Scheme in East Galway' in J. O'Sullivan and M. Stanley (eds), *New Routes to the Past* (NRA; Dublin, 2007), pp.81–100

28 Raftery (1972), p.39

29 Grogan (2005), p.112

30 Raftery (1969), Raftery (1976), Mallory (1988), Grogan (1995), Cotter (1990), in Grogan (2005), p.217

31 Grogan (2005), p.121

32 *Ibid.*, p.119

33 Harding, D.W., *Hillforts: Later Prehistoric Earthworks in Britain and Ireland* (Academic Press; London, 1976); Wheeler, M. and Richardson, K.M., *Hill-Forts of Northern France* (The Society of Antiquities; London, 1956)

34 O'Sullivan, J. (2007), pp.89-90

35 Raftery, B., *Pagan Celtic Ireland: The Enigma of the Irish Iron Age* (Thames and Hudson; London, 1994), p.182

36 Stout, M., *The Irish Ringfort* (Four Courts Press; Dublin, 1997), p.19

37 Collins, A.E.P., 'Excavations at Dressogagh Rath, Co Armagh', *Ulster Journal of Archaeology (UJA)*, vol.29, pp.117-129

38 McCormick, F., 'Cows, Ringforts and the Origins of Early Christian Ireland', *Emania*, vol.13 (1995), pp.33-37

39 Stout (1997), p.53

40 *Ibid.*, pp.81-2

41   Alcock, O. et al., *Archaeological Inventory of County Galway*, vol.II (Dublin; the Stationary Office, 1999), pp.363-5

42   Stout (1997), p.33

43   Lynn, C., 'Houses in Rural Ireland ad 500-1000', *UJA*, vol.57 (1994), pp.81–93

44   Kelly, F., *Early Irish Farming* (Dublin Institute of Advanced Studies; Dublin, 2000)

45   Waterman, D.M., 'A Group of Raths at Ballypalady, County Antrim', *UJA*, vol.35 (1972), pp.29–36

46   Mitchell, F., *The Irish Landscape* (Collins; London, 1976), p.189

47   Monk, M.A. and Kelleher, E. 'An Assessment for the Archaeological Evidence for Irish Corn-drying Kilns', *The Journal of Irish Archaeology*, vol.XIV (2005), pp.77–114

48   O'Donovan, John, *Annala Rioghachta Eireann: Annals of the Kingdom of Ireland by the Four Masters, from the Earliest Period to the Year 1616* (Dublin, 1856)

49   Reeves, William, 'On the Bell of St. Patrick, Called the Clog an Edachta', *The Transactions of the Royal Irish Academy*, vol.27 (Dublin, 1886), p.6

50   O'Flanagan, Revd M., Letters containing information relative to the antiquities of the county of Galway collected during the Ordnance Survey in 1839, vol.1, typescript in 3 Vols (Bray, 1927), pp.147-8

51   O'Donovan's Ordnance Survey Letters, vol.I (1839), pp.605, 606

52   Reeves (1886), p.6

53   Stokes, Margaret, *Early Christian Art in Ireland* (Dublin, 1887), p.58

54   Lucas, A.T. 'The Social Role of Relics and Reliquaries in Ancient Ireland', *Journal of the Royal Society of Antiquaries of Ireland*, vol.116 (Dublin, 1986), p.8

55   Ó Riain, Pádraig, *Dictionary of Irish Saints* (Dublin, 2013), p.390

56   O'Flanagan (1927), p.607

57   Mac Giolla Easpaig, Donal, 'Early Ecclesiastical Settlement Names of County Galway' in G. Moran (ed.), *Galway History and Society* (Dublin, 1996), p.811

58   Sweetman, H.S., *Calendar of Documents Relating to Ireland, 1171-1251*, vol.V (1875-86), p.222

59   Nicholls, Kenneth, 'Rectory, vicarage and parish in the Western Irish Dioceses', *Journal of the Royal Society of Antiquaries*, vol.101, part 1 (Dublin, 1971), p.72

60   Nicholls, Kenneth, 'The Visitations of the Diocese of Clonfert, Tuam and Kilmacduagh, c.1565-67', *Journal of Galway Archaeological and Historical Society* (Galway, 1970), p.148

61   The Schools' Collection, vol.0045, page 0204, Woodlawn National School, Eibhlín ní Innse (teacher), www.duchas.ie

62   Kehnel, Annette, *Clonmacnois – the Church and Lands of St Ciarán: Change and Continuity in an Irish Monastic Foundation* (sixth to the sixteenth century) (Munster, 1997), p.215; Calendar of Papal Letters XV, p.831

63   Twemlow, J.A. (ed.), *Calendar of Letters Relating to Great Britain and Ireland*, vol.10, 1447-1455, Nicolas V [Reg. Lat. 474: 26 October 1451] (1915)

64   Twemlow, J.A. (ed.), *Calendar of Papal Registers Relating to Great Britain and*

Ireland, vol.14, 1484-1492, Innocent VIII [Reg. Lat. 951: 10 August 1493] (1960)

65 Cunniffe, Christy, 'Interpreting the Stones: The Archaeology of the Medieval Parish Church at Clonbern' in E. Mullally (ed.), *Clonbern Graveyard: Its Monuments & People* (Belfast, 2011), pp.47-51; Cunniffe, Christy, 'The Early History of Clonberne Parish' in J. Kelly (ed.), *Our Lady of Mount Carmel Clonberne 1862–2012* (Ireland, 2012), pp.9-17; Cunniffe, Christy, 'An Assessment of the Archaeological and Historical Background to Killimor Medieval Parish Church', in A. Geoghegan & N. McGann (eds), *Killimor: Our Parish and Our People* (2013), pp.10-24; Cunniffe, Christy, 'All is Not Lost – the Medieval Parish Church of Donanaghta', in J. Fenwick (ed.), *Lost and Found III* (Bray, forthcoming)

66 Hayman, Richard, *A Concise Guide to the Parish Church* (Stroud, 2007), p.25

67 Ó Lochlainn, Colm, 'Roadways in Ancient Ireland', in J. Ryan (ed.), *Féil-sgríbhinn Eóin Mhic Néill: Essays and Studies Presented to Professor Eóin Mhic Néill on the Occasion of his Seventieth Birthday* (Dublin, 1940), pp.465-74; Doran, Linda, 'Medieval Communication Routes through Longford and Roscommon and their associated Settlements', *Proceedings of the Royal Irish Academy*, Section C, 104 (Dublin, 2004), pp.57–80

68 Geissel, Hermann, *A Road on the Long Ridge: In Search of the Ancient Highway on the Esker Riada* (Newbridge, 2006), p.99

69 Mac Giolla, Choille, *Books of Survey and Distribution*, vol.3 (Dublin, 1962), p.147

70 Swan, Leo, 'Enclosed Ecclesiastical Sites and their Relevance to the Settlement Patterns of the First Millennium ad' in T. Reeves-Smyth and T. Hamond (eds), *Landscape Archaeology in Ireland*, BAR British Series 116 (Oxford, 1983); Etienne Rynne, 'Leo Swan's Pet Subject: Enclosed Ecclesiastical Sites in Ireland' in T. Condit and C. Corlett (eds), *Above and Beyond: Essays in Memory of Leo Swan* (Bray, 2005)

71 Olive Alcock, Kathy de hÓra, & Paul Gosling, *Archaeological Inventory for County Galway vol.II* (Dublin, 1999), p.344

72 O'Flanagan (1927), p.148

73 Alcock et.al. (1999), p.344

74 O'Flanagan (1927), p.147

75 Mc Neill, Maura, *The Festival of Lughnasa* (Oxford, 1983), pp.39, 625

76 The Schools' Collection, vol.0045, p.0212, Woodlawn National School, Eibhlín ní Innse (teacher), www.duchas.ie

77 This article is a condensed version of one previously published in the 2011 edition of the Galway Archaeological and Historical Journal. It includes additional information about the effects of the Famine on the estate.

78 *Dublin Journal*, Saturday 26 June 1725, issue XXV

79 Berry, H.F., *A History of the Royal Dublin Society* (1915), p.27

80 Bagshaw Muniments, John Rylands Library (1721-44), Sir James Caldwell Relations BAG/3/14/1-161, nd

81 Flynn, J.S., *Ballymacward: The Story of an East Galway Parish* (privately printed, 1991), p.89

82 Register of Deeds, vol.171 (1754), p.179 (thanks to Mr Patrick Melvin)

83 *Lloyd's Evening Post and British Chronicle* (London, England), Monday 6 March 6 1758, issue 99

84 *Op cit.* Bagshaw Muniments

85 House of Commons Sessional papers; *Reports of Commissioners, 1813-1814, The third report of the commissioners appointed to enquire into the nature and extent of the several bogs in Ireland, and, the practicability of draining and cultivating them*, paper number 130, vol.VI, pt.I.1, Cockton Title: Coms. of Inquiry into Nature and Extent of Bogs in Ireland, Third Report, Appendix, chair/author: Foster, John Leslie

86 Watson, S., *The Gentleman's and Citizen's Almanack* (Dublin, 1770), p.71

87 *Op cit.* Flynn, J.S. (1991), p.186

88 Hutton, A.W. (ed.), *Arthur Young's Tour in Ireland (1776-1779)* (Irish University Press, 1970)

89 Hampshire Record Office, Letter from Charles St George to his mother, Melesina Trench 23M93/15/1/12 (1808)

90 Wikipedia, 2010, Capability Brown, available at <http://en.wikipedia.org/wiki/Lancelot_%22Capability%22_Brown>

91 Craig, M.J. and Craig, M., *Mausolea Hibernia* (Lilliput Press, 1999), pp.112-13

92 Cooke-Trench, T.R.F., *A Memoir of the Trench Family* (privately printed, 1897), pp.140-153

93 Lewis, Samuel, *A Topographical Dictionary of Ireland, Vol 2* (London: S. Lewis & Co., 1837), p.69

94 *Ibid*, pp.140-53

95 Inglis, Henry D., *A Journey throughout Ireland, during the Spring, Summer, and Autumn of 1834*, 4th edition (Whittaker; London, 1836), pp.16-20

96 Material from the Beinecke Library, Yale University, call number: OSB MSS 50, title: Ballitore papers, dates: 1709-1827, request box 6 6 Trench, Melesina (Chenevix), 1768-1827. ca. 300 ALS to Mary Leadbeater, [v.p.] 3 folders 1802 June-1827 July, 9 July 1812 (in Charles' handwriting) second part of letter is identified as being from Moira Place, Southampton, 2 July.

97 Lewis, S., *Topographical Dictionary of Ireland* (1837), p.124.

98 Commons Sessional Papers, paper number: 130, vol.VI, Pt.I.1, Cockton, title: Coms. of Inquiry into Nature and Extent of Bogs in Ireland, Third Report, Appendix, chair/author: Foster, John Leslie.

99 The Devon Commission, *Digest of evidence taken before Her Majesty's Commissioners of inquiry into the state of the law and practice in respect to the occupation of land in Ireland* (A. Thom; Dublin, 1848), p.1103-72.

100 House of Commons, *Reports of the Irish Poor Law Commissioners*, Appendix B, vol.xxxii (1845)

101 Ashtown, Lord, Letter to the Chief Secretary's Office dated 19 June 1822, available online at www.csorp.nationalarchives.ie/search/index.php?simpleSearchSbm=true&category=27&searchDescTxt=ashtown&simpleSearchSbm=Search#searchfocus

102 House of Commons, vol.36, Census of Ireland 1851, available online at http://books.google.co.uk/books?id=uPejqKxcEjIC&pg=PA792&dq=1851+census+of+ireland,+galway,+killaan&hl=en&sa=X&ei=NwgPVIfTFseL7AawpYAw&ved=0CD0Q6AEwAA#v=onepage&q=1851%20census%20of%20ireland%2C%20galway%2C%20killaan&f=false

103 Stevenson, George J., *Methodist Worthies: Characteristic Sketches of Methodist Preachers of the Several Denominations, with Historical Sketch of each Connexion*, vol.2 (T.C. Jack, 1886), p.509

104 *Surrey Comet*, Saturday 2 May 1863

105 *Tuam Herald*, 31 July 1841

106 House of Lords, Sessional Papers of the House of Lords 1854-55, vol.XXI, p.101.

107 *Freeman's Journal*, 10 March 1845

108 National Library of Ireland, cashbook of Frederick Mason Trench, 2nd Baron Ashtown 1849-1850, MS 1764

109 House of Commons, Royal Commission on Congestion in Ireland, The British Parliamentary Papers, XXXVI (1907)

110 The National Archives of Ireland, *Famine Relief Commission Papers*, 1844–1847, RFLC3/1/3708, Incoming Letters

111 The National Archives of Ireland, *Famine Relief Commission Papers*, 1844–1847, RFLC3/M/5339, Incoming Letters

112 Masterson, Josephine, 1999,1841/1851 Census Abstracts (Republic of Ireland), Genealogical Publishing Company, 1999

113 *Ibid.*

114 *Op. cit.* Cooke-Trench, T.R.F., *A Memoir of the Trench Family* (privately printed, 1897), p.154.

115 *Ibid.*

116 *The Irish Times*, 15 September 1879

117 Galway County Council Archives: Ballinasloe Poor Law Union Collection, Board of Guardians Meetings, GO0/5/A/June-October 1849

118 *Ibid.*, GO0/5/A/February-April 1850

119 HC, *Annual report of the Local Government Board for Ireland, being the eight report under 'the Local Government Board (Ireland) Act'*, 35 & 36 Vic., c. 19. 1880 [C. 2603] [C. 2603-I], XXVIII.1, 39, p.114

120 *Freeman's Journal*, 2 August 1851

121 *The Irish Times*, 19 January 1881

122 For a detailed analysis of the Land War on Clanricarde's estate see Anne Finnegan, The Land War in South-East Galway, 1879-1890 (Thesis MA: University College Galway, 1994)

123 HC, *Agrarian and other crimes (Ireland): Return relating to agrarian and other crimes (Ireland). Part II. – For the month of November 1880*, (4-1), LXXVII.151 (1881), p.41

124 *Irish Independent*, 2 October 1907

125 *Freeman's Journal*, 5 April 1894

126 *The Irish Times*, 6 January 1894

127 *Ibid.*, 8 March 1894

128 *Freeman's Journal*, 22 January 1894

129 *Ibid.*, 8 April 1899

130 *Ibid.*, 18 April 1899

131 For a detailed background into the UIL see Fergal Campbell, *Land and Revolution: Nationalist Politics in the West of Ireland, 1891-1921* (Oxford; Oxford University Press, 2005), pp.8-42

132 John Cunningham, '"Waiting for the promised money": Trade Unions in County Galway, 1890-1914' in Gerard Moran, Raymond Gillespie and William Nolan (eds), *Galway: History & Society* (Dublin; Geography Publications, 1996), pp.533-5

133 Campbell, *Land and Revolution* (2005), pp.64-9

134 *Irish Independent*, 19 May 1905

135 Campbell (2005), p.148

136 HC, *Royal Commission on Congestion in Ireland. Appendix to the tenth report. Minutes of evidence (taken in Counties Galway and Roscommon, 18th September, to 4th October, 1907), and documents relating thereto* [Cd. 4007] (1908), pp.176-185.

137 *Irish Independent*, 26 September 1907

138 *Ibid.*, 17 August 1907

139 *Ibid.*, 3 April 1908

140 Lord Ashtown (ed.), *The Unknown Power behind the Irish Nationalist Party: Its Present Work and Criminal History* (Swan Sonneshein & Co; London, 1908)

141 *The Irish Times*, 5 November 1908

142 *Grievances from Ireland*, vol.VI, No. 60, January 1910, p.5

143 *Irish Independent*, 18 May 1912

144 *Ibid.*, 28 January 1913

145 *Connacht Tribune*, 11 April 1914

146 *Irish Independent*, 8 June 1914

147 *Ibid.*, 27 February 1918

148 Terence Dooley, *The Decline of the Big House in Ireland: A Study of Irish Landed Families* (Dublin; Wolfhound Press, 2001), p.143

149 *The Irish Times*, 21 May 1920

150 *Connacht Tribune*, 31 July 1920

151 Lewis Perry Curtis, 'The Last Gasp of Southern Unionism: Lord Ashtown of Woodlawn', *Eire-Ireland*, vol.40:3&4 (Fall/Winter 2005), p.181

152 *Connacht Tribune*, 21 January 1922

153 Mercer, B., 'The History of Woodlawn Estate, 1550-1800', *Journal of the*

Galway Archaeological and Historical Society, vol.63 (2011), pp.77

154 *Ibid.*, p.78

155 Bence-Jones, M., *A Guide to Irish Country Houses* (1988), p.xiii

156 Craig, M., The Architecture of Ireland from the earliest times to 1880 (1982), p.180

157 Bence-Jones, M. (1988), p.xv

158 Mercer, B. (2011), vol.63, pp.73-87

159 National Library Prints & Drawings, AD3590

160 Bence Jones, M. (1988), p.xix

161 Girourard, M., *Life in the English Country House* (1994), p.208

162 Rothery, S., *A Field Guide to the Buildings of Ireland* (1997), p.166

163 Dictionary of Irish Architects 1720-1940 Irish Architectural Archive [online], www.dia.ie [Accessed 3 March, 2015]

164 *Ibid.*, p.165.

165 O'Donovan, J., *Ordnance Survey Field Name Books* (1838)

166 Dictionary of Irish Architects 1720-1940 Irish Architectural Archive [online], www.dia.ie [Accessed 3 March, 2015]

167 www.emigrationisle.com

168 Irwin, Benjamin, *The Journal of the Association for the Preservation of Memorials of the Dead in Ireland*, vol.2 (1895)

169 Hurlbert, William Henry, *Ireland Under Coercion: The Diary of an American*, p.160

170 We spell the name Cregg here, the same as in the census. It is also spelled Craig, as in Woodlawn school registration book

171 Watson, S., *The Gentleman's and Citizens Almanack* (Dublin, 1770)

172 National Archives, Dublin – ED1/33/35 National School Records

173 National Archives, Dublin – ED1/34/76/2B

174 The 'inches' would refer to the measurement on a map

175 National Archives, Dublin – ED/2/140

176 The following files are among those consulted with the kind permission and assistance of staff at The National Archives, Dublin: ED1/33 No. 35, ED1/34/76/2B, ED1/34 No. 76, ED2/2/18, ED/2/140, ED1/37 No. 275, ED/9/3822, ED9/14902, ED2/37/275

177 Woodlawn N.S., Index of Registry for Boys & Girls from 1886 were consulted with kind permission and assistance of Principal Ms Edel Dwyer, Secretery Ann Earls and Parish Priest Fr Pat Kenny

178 We would like to acknowledge the assistance and co-operation of former staff and pupils of Woodlawn National School for their contribution of information and photographic material for this publication.

179 Interview with Michael Carney, 18/08/2010

180 Letters were contributed and reproduced courtesy of Mary Dempsey (*née* Kelly, Carrahulla, Woodlawn)

SELECT BIBLIOGRAPHY AND FURTHER READING

BOOKS AND ARTICLES

Alcock, Olive, Kathy de hÓra & Paul Gosling, *Archaeological Inventory for County Galway*, vol.II (Dublin, 1999)

Archaeology Ireland, published quarterly by Wordwell Press

Bence-Jones, M., *A Guide to Irish Country Houses* (1988)

Bence-Jones, M., *'Life in an Irish Country House'*, History and Politics Series Illustrated Edition (Constable, 1996)

Bennett, I., 'Excavations Bulletin', www.excavations.ie

Blake, Tarquin, *Abandoned Mansions of Ireland Volume 2* (2013)

Campbell, Fergal, *Land and Revolution: Nationalist Politics in the West of Ireland, 1891-1921* (Oxford; Oxford University Press, 2005)

Carson, Charles John Thomas, *Technology and the Big House in Ireland, c. 1800-c. 1930* (Cambria Press, 2009)

Collins, T. and Coyne, F., 'A Mesolithic Cemetery – Ireland's Oldest Burials' http://irisharchaeology.ie/2013/03/a-mesolithic-cemetery-irelands-oldest-burials/#sthash.wTLDW2wW.dpuf) (2003 & 2006)

Cooke-Trench, T.R.F., *A Memoir of the Trench Family* (privately printed, 1897)

Craig, M., *The Architecture of Ireland from the Earliest Times to 1880* (Dublin; Eason, 1982)

Curtis, Lewis Perry, 'The Last Gasp of Southern Unionism: Lord Ashtown of Woodlawn in Eire-Ireland', vol.40:3&4, Fall/Winter (2005)

Dooley, Terence, *The Decline of the Big House in Ireland: A Study of Irish Landed Families* (Dublin; Wolfhound Press, 2001)

Dooley, Terence and Christopher Ridgway (eds), *The Irish Country House: Its Past, Present and Future* (Four Courts Press, 2015)

Flynn, J.S., *Ballymacward – The Story of an East Galway Parish* (Ireland, 1991)

Grogan, E., *The North Munster Project*, vol.2 (Wordwell; Bray, 2005)

Hennessy, Ronán, Martin Feely, Christy Cunniffe and Caitriona Carlin, *Galway's Living Landscapes – Part 1; Eskers* (Galway County Council, 2010)

Mc Neill, Maura, *The Festival of Lughnasa* (Oxford, 1983)

Melvin, Patrick, *Estates and Landed Society in Galway* (Dublin: Éamonn de Búrca, 2012)

Mercer, Bríd, 'History of the Woodlawn estate: 1550-1800' in *Journal of the Galway Archaeological and Historical Society*, LXIII (2011), pp.73-87

O'Donovan, John, *Annala Rioghachta Eireann: Annals of the Kingdom of Ireland by the Four Masters, from the Earliest Period to the Year 1616* (Dublin, 1856)

O'Sullivan, J., *The Quiet Landscape: Archaeological Discoveries on a Road Scheme in East Galway* (National Roads Authority, 2007)

Perry Curtis, Lewis, 'The Last Gasp of Southern Unionism: Lord Ashtown of Woodlawn', *Eire-Ireland*, vol.40:3&4, Fall/Winter (2005), p.181

Powell, P., *Megalithic Monuments of Ireland, County Guide Series Volume XVI Galway* (2012)

Raftery, B., 'Irish Hillforts', in C. Thomas (ed.), *The Irish Sea Provence*, CBA Research Report 9 (Council for British Archaeology; London, 1972), pp.37-58

Raftery, B., *Pagan Celtic Ireland – The Enigma of the Irish Iron Age* (Thames and Hudson; London, 2000)

Reeves, William, 'On the Bell of St. Patrick, Called the Clog an Edachta', *The Transactions of the Royal Irish Academy*, vol.27 (Dublin, 1886), p.6

Rothery, S., *A Field Guide to the Buildings of Ireland – Illustrating the Smaller Buildings of Town & Countryside* (Dublin; Lilliput, 1997)

Ryan, M. 'An Early Mesolithic site in the Irish Midlands', *Antiquity*, vol.54 (1980), pp.46-7 online at http://heritagecouncil.ie/unpublished_exavations/section3.html.

Ryan, M., *Irish Archaeology Illustrated* (Country House Dublin, 1994)

Somerville-Large, Peter, *The Irish Country House: A Social History* (Sinclair-Stevenson, 1995)

Stout, M., *The Irish Ringfort* (Four Courts Press; Dublin, 1997)

The Schools' Collection, Woodlawn National School, Eibhlín ní Innse (teacher), vol.45, p.204

Waddell, J., *The Prehistoric Archaeology of Ireland* (Wordwell, 2010)

WEBSITES

www.archaeology.ie

www.duchas.ie

www.excavations.ie

www.galwaycommunityheritage.org

www.irisharchaeology.ie

INDEX

Trench, Godolphin 56
Tuam 44, 49, 90, 103, 106, 127, 130
Tullawicky 15, 60, 92
Turlough Hill, County Clare 33
Turner, Francis 105
Turoe 25
Tyrellspass 103

Ua Dubhagáin (O'Doogan), John 45
United States of America 67, 75, 88, 92, 121
Urraghry, Ballinasloe 18

Victoria, Queen 103
Vaughan, Evan 102

Wakefield 57
Walsh, Minnie 67
Ward, Paddy Joe 90
Waterford 12, 64, 66, 69, 75

Webb, James Henry 79
Westland Row Station, Dublin 90
Whitepark 95
William III, King 52
William IV, King 103
Witherings, Thomas 102
Woodlawn
   Church 5, 12, 57, 85, 86, 87, 142
   Estate 5, 14, 16, 52, 55, 62, 71, 85, 131, 134
   House 5, 12, 52, 53, 54, 61, 71, 72, 73, 74, 75, 76, 77, 78, 79, 80, 81, 82, 83, 84, 85, 93, 108,
   Post-office 5, 15, 103, 104, 105, 107
   School 8, 15, 16, 51, 53, 105, 108 - 119, 127, 128, 131, 132
   Station 26, 83, 88-97, 120
Woodman, Professor 18

Young, Arthur 54, 129